Contents

The Hidden RADIANCE

Unveiling the Untold Saga of a Quiet YOGI

SRI SADHGURU PARAMAHAMSA NAGA YOGI RAJ

(Dr C. NAGARAJ)

Compilation and Transcreation

By

DR. HARI CHINTHAKUNTA

Dedication

Avadootha NANNA and Karunamayi AMMA

This book is profoundly dedicated to the sacred Lotus Feet of our revered parents, whose divine perception transcends the ordinary. They possess a celestial insight into who we truly are, why we are here, and the sacred mission we are destined to fulfil on this earthly journey. With unparalleled grace, they endured life's adversities, bearing their trials with serene smiles that belied their suffering. Their unwavering commitment to elevating our spirits and enriching our lives exemplifies the highest form of selfless love.

Their love, a universal embrace, transcends caste, and creed, manifesting as a boundless compassion that sees beyond superficial distinctions. They never compared us to others or questioned the timing of life's delays, for they understood that such moments were not denials but divine interventions, preserving something uniquely precious for us. They viewed rituals and prayers not merely as traditions but as sacred practices that reconnect us with the Divine, honour our ancestors, and acknowledge the benevolent forces that have shaped our lives. Through these practices, they equipped us to withstand the onslaughts of time and navigate the intricate journey of inner transformation. Their eternal spirit continues to guide and protect us, illuminating our path as we endeavour to fulfil our divine mission. With every step we take, we strive to embody their virtues of humility, honesty, and heartfelt dedication, ever mindful that our journey is a sacred offering to the Almighty, detached from the fruits of our actions.

Dr. Hari, Chinthakunta

A Tribute to Timeless Light

Who can fill the void you left?
Where are you now, I wonder?
Your presence was clear when I could see you,
And even when my eyes were closed, you shone.
Your light was divine,
And your majesty revealed itself in full.
From the start, you taught me the values of life,
Guiding us to follow a divine path,
Your generosity was unmatched,
And your sacrifice was always evident.
In everything you did, you gave selflessly,
Your deep spirituality was always bright,
You revealed hidden truths through your silent grace,
A testament to your profound inner light.
You were like a mother, father, and friend to me,
A guide, philosopher, and healer,
Your presence was a steady beacon,
A vast spirit that embraced us all.
You were unique and fulfilled in every way,
Your flawlessness and pure heart shone brightly.
Your words were always truthful,

Your memory remains with me,

A bond of deep affection,

A lasting fragrance of love.

In your presence, there was a gentle grace,

A pure, childlike heart,

Unaffected by the world's troubles,

And the wisdom of a seasoned yogi.

Simplicity was your guiding star,

Connecting us through time and space,

In every moment, you were calm and wise.

How can we fully understand your depth?

Where timeless truths and shadows meet,

A child's innocence combined with a sage's wisdom,

In your silence, the mysteries unfolded.

After you left suddenly, I felt lost,

Disappointed and as if abandoned,

But deep inside, I felt a message:

You are still watching over me, giving me strength.

You guide me to write about you,

To share your story and your grand love,

Your love is a bright flame,

Keeping my spirits alive and warm.

Bless me with your smiles, banish my fear,

Heal my mind, body, and soul from within,

Fill me with divine energy, pure and clear,

And help me fulfil the path Nature has pinned.

Dr. Hari

Preface

In the grand tapestry of existence, where every soul weaves its sacred pattern into the cosmic dance of creation and dissolution, the story of Dr C. Nagaraj stands as a beacon of profound wisdom and spiritual depth. His diaries, rich with timeless truths and divine love, transformed our home into a sanctuary of enlightenment. This narrative seeks to immortalize his spiritual legacy, shedding light on the path to awakening for all seekers.

Life's journey, as Dr. Nagaraj's writings reveal, is more than a mere passage of time; it is a sacred odyssey of spiritual discovery. Each step we take unveils the boundless depths of our souls and the greatest exploration lies within—not in traversing external landscapes but in delving into the infinite expanse of our inner being.

The pages that follow capture the essence of Dr. Nagaraj's profound journey—his spiritual odyssey meticulously compiled from his life's works. These writings reverberate with timeless wisdom and enlightenment. My quest to document his legacy was guided by diligent research and the whispers of intuition. I honoured his profound spiritual quest with the title Sri Sadguru Paramahamsa Naga Yogi Raj, a testament to his deep spiritual journey.

Selecting from his extensive writings, accumulated over five decades, proved challenging. I intend to share these insights with those who seek to grow internally and excel in inner engineering. My journey with him, spanning nearly six decades, unveiled subtle truths about life and spirituality. His simplicity, honesty, truth, love, and empathy reached Himalayan heights. Despite his profound spiritual experiences and interactions with revered spiritual masters, he remained grounded and unassuming. He never claimed greatness but instead maintained a low profile, firmly believing that God elevates those who humble themselves.

Although he never openly disclosed it, his writings and shared insights subtly reveal his association with the esteemed Himalayan saints. Dr. Nagaraj's nature was not confined to any single religious system; his essence embraced all religious ideologies and philosophies. His interactions with me, especially towards the end of his life, unveiled subtle truths he had kept to himself. His diaries speak volumes of his journey, yet he never sought to publish his articles or life history.

His physical departure on August 3, 2022, left a significant void. Although he had hinted at his imminent departure, the reality of his absence was profound. This prompted me to delve deeply into his extensive diaries and writings—works he had never disclosed until his last breath. It is through his grace that I undertook this sacred task of compilation and transcreation. Despite my initial apprehension, his divine guidance illuminated my path, making the task manageable and fulfilling.

I also extend my heartfelt gratitude to my parents and my only sister, now in heaven, for their invisible guidance throughout this noble endeavour. My younger brother, Ganesh, and my cousin Prathima's silent support provided additional strength and encouragement during this journey. Special thanks to Sree Lekha, Sai Leela, and Uma Devi for the proofreading.

This book is a humble tribute to a great brother—a true yogi, friend, philosopher, and a perfect human being who never lied, even in jest. It is a heartfelt offering, born from a deep wellspring of affection for a brother whose divine presence graced my life. It is also an opportunity to reflect on my association with him and to illuminate the story of a simple person with profoundly high thinking.

May these pages serve as a beacon of light, illuminating the path to spiritual awakening and guiding souls toward the truths of existence. Through his profound teachings and the quiet wisdom embedded in his diaries, may readers find inspiration and guidance in their own spiritual journeys.

Dr. Hari

Foreword

It is with deep reverence and profound gratitude that I pen the foreword for *The Hidden Radiance: Unveiling the Untold Saga of a Quiet YOGI*. This extraordinary book illuminates the life of my brother—an unparalleled mentor, guide, and the living embodiment of divine grace. His existence was a testament to a life lived in perfect harmony with the divine, radiating wisdom, compassion, and spiritual depth.

My brother was a living paradox—a childlike innocence intertwined with the profound wisdom of ages. His presence was both a gentle whisper from the divine and a clarion call to deeper understanding. His writings, spanning poetry and prose in both English and Telugu, resonate with a spirituality that transcends the mundane. From his early years, he harboured a deep passion for poetry, a passion that evolved alongside his spiritual journey. He travelled with various spiritual masters, whose teachings shaped his understanding and connected him with the roots of his divine heritage.

In his professional life, my elder brother served as both a doctor and a lecturer at the Government Medical College. He was a beacon of inspiration, guiding medical students with his dedication and compassion. His commitment to medicine and teaching exemplified a life devoted to service and learning. As Albert Einstein wisely observed, "A person who never made a mistake never tried anything new." My brother's life, marked by a continual quest for knowledge and self-improvement, demonstrated that true fulfilment arises from selfless service and unwavering dedication.

In his medical practice, he was a paragon of selfless service, treating patients without concern for monetary gain. His expertise in Homeopathy was driven by a divine vision of holistic healing—a vision aimed at bringing solace to those in suffering. Although his physical presence is no longer with us, his spiritual essence continues to guide and inspire.

My second brother, Dr. Hari, embraced the role of caretaker for our parents and attended to all the family's needs with unwavering devotion. Even as he bore these responsibilities alone, he did so with a spirit immersed in divine contemplation, embodying the essence of service and devotion. As Saint Francis of Assisi beautifully expressed, "For it is in giving that we receive." Dr. Hari's selfless acts are a testament to this profound truth.

The compilation of this book by Dr. Hari is a divine act of grace. Through his exploration of our elder brother's diaries and writings—preserved in quietude even from us—he has unveiled a wellspring of wisdom. My elder brother's life was marked by humility, reflecting the belief that "Those who humble themselves shall be exalted" (Matthew 23:12). As Sri Ramakrishna Paramahamsa profoundly stated, "He who has realized the Self sees all beings in himself, and himself in all beings." His spiritual dialogues with Dr. Hari, alongside his introduction to the teachings of Paramahamsa Rama Krishna and Paramahamsa Yogananda, profoundly influenced our understanding. Despite enduring immense personal grief—losing my sister, our parents, and himself struggling with his own health—he withstood the pain with remarkable resilience.

As you delve into this book, you may find yourself journeying into a realm of profound reflection and divine connection. As Jalaluddin Rumi, the 13th-century Persian poet and mystic, beautifully said, "Let yourself be silently drawn by the strange pull of what you really love. It will not lead you astray." And as the Bhagavad Gita reveals, "He who has attained the knowledge of the Self sees all beings in himself, and himself in all beings" (Bhagavad Gita 6:29).

I feel proud to have been born into such a noble family, where each member, including our parents, brothers, and sister, seems to have travelled together from previous lives, each soul a source of joy and each suffering moving the others. It is as if the same soul resided in six bodies, bound by an unbreakable spiritual connection.

Let me pray to God that this book reaches as many spiritual aspirants as possible and helps them find answers to their unanswered questions. May it offer you joy, peace, and a transformative perspective on life.

Ganesh, Chinthakunta

The Eternal Light of Amma's Love: A Cry from the Heart

*Celebrating the Unconditional Love of
Our Beloved Mother*

Dr Hari, Chinthakunta

Introduction: A Tribute to Amma's Eternal Spirit

After the demise of our beloved mother on 28th August 2015, life felt empty, and we could not bear her separation. The void left behind seemed unbearable, and the pain of her absence lingered in every corner of my heart. I often remembered the nights I slept beside her, caressing her hand, and it was during these moments of deep longing that I compiled nine melodious songs as a tribute to her love and care. This Telugu album, *Amma Telugu Album 2013* (available on YouTube here), was the first of its kind—a collection of nine songs representing the nine months we spent in our mother's womb, protected and nurtured by her relentless love.

The tears have never truly stopped, the feelings remain unerased, and my heart continues to feel heavy with her absence. One day, without my knowledge, I found myself writing a beautiful lyric. It was then that I realized something extraordinary—my hands were moving, guided by thoughts that I could only attribute to my mother's spirit. I felt her presence, strong and clear, though her beautiful physical form was no longer with me. That moment made me aware that she had never truly left. Her spirit lives on, guiding me in ways beyond comprehension.

Through all of this, my brother, Naga Yogi Raj, has been my unwavering source of solace, embodying the deep love of our Amma, our father Nanna, and our dear sister. His presence has given me the strength to carry on, keeping alive the bond that unites us, even in the face of our losses. When he departed from this world on 3rd August 2022, it created a profound void in my life. In that moment of grief, I came to understand the impermanence of life, and I resolved to move forward, embracing the role that Nature has assigned me. The painful moment in my life triggered me to take up the task of compiling a book entitled **"The Hidden Radiance- Unveiling the Untold Saga of a Quiet YOGI."**

This piece is a dedication to all the mothers—those who have seen me, those who have not, and those watching over me from the Earth and Heaven. With deep humility, I bow before all mothers, seeking their blessings as I share this tribute, hoping to touch millions of hearts that carry the sacred love of a mother. Let us always cherish and honour the presence of mothers, for they are the living embodiment of unconditional love. I am forever grateful for their selfless devotion.

Our Compassionate Mother

Amma! The one gift we received from you, which never allowed another desire to arise in our hearts, is that eternal, pure, divine motherly love! Amma! The  loss that nothing could ever fill—your incomparable, unmatched, wonderful flow of motherly affection showered upon us! Once we received the boundless, eternal place you lovingly envisioned for us in the throne of your love, there was never a thought of climbing any other summit.

In this Kali Yuga, where the mechanical and deceitful love of the world prevails, you shielded us from its grasp, nurturing us under your warm wings and guiding us constantly on the path of righteousness. You are none other than the Goddess of Dharma!

Though physical ailments weighed heavily on you, and time cast you into oceans of sorrow and trials, it could never shake the mountains of your patience, weaken your mental fortitude, or breach the vastness of your spiritual world. Your radiant smile always danced on your lips, reminding us of your indomitable spirit.

Amma, the Heart of Our Lives

Our soul bond—how ancient, how timeless—who knows its origin? In us, you exist. In you, we exist. With us, you are. With you, we are. In each other, we find ourselves. This is our world, ours alone.

No matter how many ages pass, separation is impossible. This is the undeniable truth witnessed by the gods, the mystery of creation unknown to the world. You are the force that lives on in us, guiding our every step, filling our hearts with love that transcends time itself.

Amma! Your divine form forever lives in our hearts, offering us visions of hope and warmth at every moment. The inseparable bond of affection fills us with spiritual nectar; your loving eyes illuminate new lights, dispelling the darkness of ignorance and igniting the flame of wisdom. Your gentle scoldings, always reigning in our restless senses, guide us along the path of service.

The Comfort of Your Love

Your smiling face, amidst the waves of despair, instils enthusiasm within us, filling us with breaths of hope in this battle of life. Your cool blessings stand as a shield, protecting us from falling into the clutches of harmful forces. Your tender lips brush our cheeks with lullabies, comforting us with love. Your hand of assurance wipes our tears, feeding us with tender care, and your lotus feet, like holy pilgrimages, grant us divine experiences.

Amma! Your words of nectar resound in our hearts, awakening us to our highest potential. Your patience, deeper than oceans, helps us uncover pearls of wisdom in the sea of hardships. You offer your hand of grace to guide us to shore, urging us to embrace universal love and freeing us from the thorny chains of narrow attachments.

The Guiding Light of Your Presence

Your heartbeat awakens us from the slumber of illusion, preparing us for our duties with steadfast commitment. Though your physical form is beyond our reach, your essence surrounds us, whispering through the wind and guiding us in the stillness of our hearts. Each tear that falls from our eyes touches your feet in heaven. Every beat of our hearts echoes your name, for your love fuels our very existence.

What else can we offer, Amma, but to remember you until our last heartbeat? Your grace flows like sacred rivers that nourish life, while your love is the light that cuts through our darkest hours. The beauty of your presence, like a compass, shows us the way in the vast sea of life, while kisses planted on your soft forehead leave us spellbound. Your gentle laughter enchants us, filling us with bliss.

Timeless Guidance

Amma! Your wise words are etched forever on the slate of our hearts, becoming timeless guides in life. Your silence corrects the rhythms of our lives, refining our values and unveiling the deeply ingrained humanity within us. In your playful mockery, we rediscover our childhood, drawing us closer to embrace you. Your steadfast attitude breaks the bonds of superstition and ignorance, guiding us toward wisdom and discernment.

Who else but you earnestly desire our well-being in this world? Who else but you forgive our mistakes and listen to our prayers? Who else but you senses and consoles our deepest griefs? Who else but you can extinguish our raging sorrows and give us peace?

The Eternal Spirit of Amma

Amma! You are the great Yogini we encountered, the great wise one we touched, the compass of our lives, and the wondrous sculptor who continually moulds us. You receive our heartfelt offerings in this home of ours, and you are the eternal spirit that guides us. You are the source of the strength within us.

Even if time separates us, you transcend it—you will always be our mother, the mother above all mothers. You are the light of countless stars in the sky of our souls. We, who were breathed into existence within your womb, are blessed, born with purpose. We are the delicate flowers blossoming in the garden of values you nurtured.

A Life Dedicated to You

This life you have given us is dedicated to you. To fulfil your vision, we rededicate ourselves. Enjoying the love you shared, savouring the memories, we quench our thirst in your ocean of compassion like swans—eternal, blissful swans.

Amma! Your word is our life's scripture. Your path is our life's purpose. Your abode is our temple. Your service is our life's yoga. Your song is the melody of our lives. You are our world. In you, we ultimately merge.

******

A Reflection on Society: The Fate of Mothers in Modern Times

In today's fast-paced society, it is deeply deplorable that the mother who has nurtured her children with such equanimity, love, and sacrifice is often left to her fate in her old age. Some are abandoned, while others are sent to old-age homes and treated as burdens when they should be revered as pillars of our existence. Be it a father or a mother, no parent should face the loneliness of an old-age home, like orphans cast aside. This is a cruel reflection of our neglect, and we must remember that a day will come when each of us will reach old age and face the same circumstances.

Let us not forget the deep emotional balance and equanimity with which mothers raise their children, instilling stability even during the most challenging times. In this regard, it becomes even more sorrowful when they are cast away during their later years. Let us cultivate a society where our parents are cherished, honoured, and cared for as they age, for they are the foundation of our lives. By taking care of them in their final years, we honour the love and sacrifices they made for us. In this, we not only uplift our own humanity but create a world where love is passed from generation to generation—a world where no mother or father is left behind.

A Humble Call to Sons and Daughters

Let us pause amidst the chaos of our busy lives and turn our hearts toward the sacred bond we share with our mothers. They are the silent warriors, the unseen architects of our dreams, and the bearers of unconditional love. Each moment spent in their embrace is a treasure that enriches our souls, a symphony of love that reverberates through the corridors of our hearts.

Reflect on the countless sacrifices they've made, the quiet tears they've shed in moments of struggle, and the boundless joy they have given in your triumphs. In their eyes, we see reflections of our potential, and in their smiles, we find the courage to rise. Let us not take this divine connection for granted. Reach out, hold their hands, and whisper words of gratitude and love. Let them feel your presence, for nothing warms a mother's heart like the knowledge that her child cherishes her.

Remember, the day will come when the sounds of laughter and joy may be replaced by echoes of silence. Embrace them now, for each hug, word, and shared moment is a sacred gift. Let us not allow the passage of time to rob us of these precious opportunities to express our love. In nurturing this bond, we not only honour our mothers but also find our true selves—woven together in a tapestry of love that transcends time.

Cosmic Mother

Divine Insights: The Spiritual Odyssey of Dr. C. Nagaraj

In the vast expanse of spiritual exploration, each soul embarks on a unique journey that contributes to the intricate tapestry of existence. Dr. C. Nagaraj's life and writings offer a profound testament to this journey, revealing a path of divine insight and wisdom. His diaries, filled with deep spiritual reflections and timeless truths, have transformed our understanding of life and spirituality, guiding us towards a deeper connection with the divine and with ourselves.

Every soul weaves its unique thread in the grand tapestry of existence, contributing to the cosmic dance of creation and dissolution. Dr. C. Nagaraj's diaries, rich with profound wisdom and spiritual depth, have transformed our home into a sanctuary of timeless truths. Through his writings, imbued with divine love and universal interconnectedness, he offered solace and guidance amidst life's myriad challenges. This narrative immortalizes his spiritual legacy, illuminating the path to enlightenment for all seekers.

Life's journey is not merely a passage of time but a sacred odyssey of spiritual discovery. As the Bhagavad Gita reveals, "The soul is neither born nor does it die" (Gita 2.20). Each step unveils the boundless depths of our souls, for the greatest exploration lies not in traversing external landscapes but in delving into the infinite expanse of our inner being, where the secrets of the universe await revelation.

The pages before you encapsulate a profound journey—the spiritual odyssey of Dr. C. Nagaraj, meticulously compiled from his life's works. Within these depths lie the reverberations of spiritual truths, resonating with timeless wisdom and enlightenment. As the Upanishads illuminate, "In the stillness of the soul, the divine is found" (Chandogya Upanishad 3.14.1).

To trace his path, I embarked on a journey through his extensive diaries and working notes, guided by diligent research and the whispers of intuition within my soul. Thus, I anointed him with the name Sri Sadguru Paramahamsa Naga Yogi Raj—a homage to the profound depth of his spiritual quest, receiving consent from his spiritual masters.

Dr. Nagaraj's journey epitomized a rich heritage of divine connection rooted in the spiritual soil of Naga Loka. As a "Yogi," he embraced renunciation akin to a Sanyasi, while as a "Paramahamsa," he embodied enlightened discernment. The title "Raj" bestowed upon him an aura of tranquil authority akin to an emperor of peace, much like the revered sages of old.

In the tapestry of existence, each soul is a thread, weaving its unique pattern into the fabric of the cosmos. The Bhagavad Gita teaches us, "The divine essence pervades all creation" (Gita 10.20). His diaries revealed layers of wisdom and spiritual depth, turning our home into a sanctuary brimming with volumes on spirituality, the life histories of monks, and philosophical texts echoing his spiritual voyage.

Through life's paradoxes, his writings unveiled an inherent goodness, wisdom, and profound love for the divine, the universe, and humanity. Each diary entry was a sacred expression, safeguarding the sanctity of his innermost thoughts. As the Ramayana speaks of, "In adversity, the divine reveals its true form" (Yuddha Kanda 6.110.19).

During the solitude of night, he shared divine visions, imparting spiritual insights that captivated my soul. His communion with Nature during late-night walks invoked blessings from celestial bodies, revealing the interconnectedness of all life. As the ancient texts state, "Nature is a reflection of the divine" (Bhagavad Gita 9.22).

Within the stillness of nature lies the symphony of the divine, whispering secrets of eternity to those who listen with the heart. His unwavering quest for truth propelled him through life's myriad contradictions, drawing solace from the timeless wisdom passed down through the ages. Immersed in spiritual practices, his profound connection with the plant and animal kingdoms reflected a deep reverence for all living beings, symbolizing the intricate web of interconnectedness woven throughout existence.

In the silent embrace of nature, we discover the rhythm of our heartbeat, echoing the pulse of the universe. His journey alongside Yogis and divine beings hinted at a timeless connection forged across lifetimes. Despite the allure of worldly pursuits, he remained steadfast in his devotion to spiritual growth, as the Bhagavad Gita counsels, "Seek the divine within, and all will be revealed" (Gita 6.6).

The path he trod was not without challenges—discrimination, unfulfilled aspirations, and personal loss marked his journey. Yet, his spirit remained unyielding, radiating love and guidance to all who crossed his path. As the Upanishads remind us, "In the face of adversity, true wisdom blooms" (Isha Upanishad 12).

In documenting his life's narrative, my intention is not merely to exalt his name but to enshrine his legacy of love, wisdom, and spiritual insight. This work is a humble tribute, born from a profound wellspring of affection and reverence for a brother whose divine presence has illuminated my life. It is an offering to the world, crafted with care to reflect the essence of his spiritual journey and the deep connections he forged with the divine and with humanity.

As the Bhagavad Gita teaches, "One who has unwavering faith in the divine, and who sees the divine presence in all things, achieves true wisdom" (Gita 12.2). Dr. Nagaraj's life was a testament to this teaching. His journey was not merely an individual pursuit but a beacon of hope and guidance for all who seek to understand the deeper truths of existence. His spiritual odyssey reminds us that each of us is on a path of discovery, where every experience, whether joyous or challenging, is a step towards greater enlightenment.

May these pages serve as a radiant beacon, guiding those who seek spiritual awakening and illuminating the path toward a profound understanding of the eternal truths. As we immerse ourselves in his wisdom, may we find our own inner light, transcending the illusions of the material world and embracing the boundless love and interconnectedness that define our true nature.

In honouring his legacy, let us strive to embody the virtues he cherished—compassion, wisdom, and unwavering faith. By doing so, we not only honour his memory but also contribute to the greater tapestry of spiritual enlightenment that binds us all. May his divine insights inspire us to embark on our spiritual journeys with renewed vigour, embracing the sacred dance of creation and dissolution with open hearts and enlightened minds.

Premonitions and Spiritual Journeys: A Brother's Tale

In the final chapter of his earthly journey, my brother, Dr Nagaraj, seemed prepared to transcend his physical form, seeking solace in sacred places and spiritual reflections. We shared late-night discussions about Himalayan saints, where he revealed his sense of being a soul on a temporary visit. His last days were marked by serene visits to peaceful temples and nature sanctuaries, where he felt a deep connection. The sudden tragedy of his passing was a profound shock, but through this, I found the strength to honour his legacy. His wisdom and love now guide me, inspiring a life of gratitude, humility, and purpose. I intend to make his hiddenly treasured autobiography, which I compiled, edited, trans-created, and organized, available to spiritual seekers, although he had confined it to himself.

Realizations of Departure

Lately, I realized that he had prepared his mind to leave his physical body and return to where he came from, taking human form to live among us. He used to insist that I take him to places like Kasapuram, Muradi, and Nimbagal, where Guru Vyasarayalu, the avatar 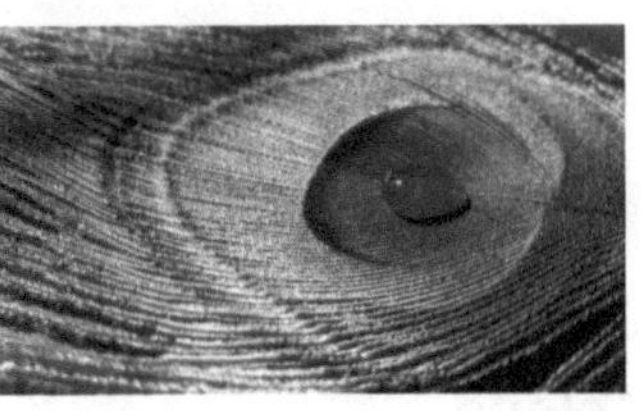 before Raghavendra Swamy of Mantralayam, had installed the idols of Lord Hanuman, his favourite deity. He also asked to visit the Sri Lakshmi Narasimha Swamy Temple in Baktharahalli and the Jilledugunta Hanuman Temple near Madakasira.

Late Night Revelations and Philosophical Talks

We often went to bed late, and he would compel me to watch videos about the lives of Himalayan saints on YouTube. Sometimes, I would fall asleep, and he would wake me, telling me to wash my face and refresh myself. He used to say, *"This is the only time we stay together. There will be none to help you, not humans, but God only and God alone."* Occasionally, he would correct my project reports late at night, then suddenly speak of his body not being able to accommodate his powerful soul. He used to frequently share that he felt like kicking his body, falling from a big hill, or walking through running waters.

He would say, "I am not what you see. I am different. I don't belong to this earth and have no work to do here, although I devised a master plan that remained unfolded for reasons best known to the one who sent me here. I came here to live with all of you and do something for your family. It is selfish to stay with this body after our parents and Vasantha left us."

Spiritual Experiences and Temple Visits

Three days **before** his passing, he asked me to take him to a place with nature and peace, free from crowds and noise. I took him to Sri Kailasam near CK Palli, which he greatly enjoyed. He said he felt like meditating there, where Saptha Rushulu did penance. While going to the place, he asked me to capture nature's photos.

When we arrived, a few dogs accompanied us, and an intellectually disabled person, who mostly stayed there, compelled us to climb the steps using signals. He took us to the peak where the samadhi of the ashram Peetadhipathi was located. An idol of Lord Krishna in a standing posture fascinated him, and he asked me to take photographs. Later, we visited a Home for the Aged, and he interacted closely with the residents.

Sudden Tragedy and Unforeseen Loss

Upon our return, I asked him what to cook. He suggested we eat the leftover food from the morning. He went to the washroom, and I assumed he was taking a bath. My driver asked if he could stay for a while, and I said there was no need. When the driver left, I searched for my brother and found him still in the bathroom, with the tap overflowing. I cried out loudly, feeling something was wrong.

When he did not respond, I broke open the door. Saileela, a rural girl who stayed with us during critical times, helped me carry him from the bathroom. He was in a sleeping posture, and I initially thought he had fallen and injured his head, but there was no visible injury or bleeding. I suspected a stroke as one side of his body was paralyzed.

My driver's family and staff arrived at midnight, and we took him to a local hospital. The doctors said there was a bleed, and he needed surgery. Though I knew the likely outcome, I accepted the surgery as others suggested it. After the surgery, my brother remained in the hospital for three days, preparing me for his departure. On August 3, 2022, he breathed his last, leaving me alone.

Legacy and Gratitude

I became deeply depressed, unable to imagine such an abrupt disappearance, especially since he was healthy and conscious of his health as a doctor. I carried him to our garden land, where my parents and sister rested permanently. It took months to digest the harsh realities of life.

I decided to read his diaries, notes, and poetry and document them as a token of gratitude. God created him, and He took him back. This experience reaffirmed the impermanency of human life. Life is God's drama, and we are merely actors who must leave after our roles are over.

A series of tragedies in our family sapped my physical and psychological energy, but I chose to live to fulfil the tasks my parents and the Almighty assigned. Until then, I keep my spirits alive, praying for the strength to perform my duties without expecting the outcome.

Embracing Life's Lessons

Reflecting on the journey shared with my brother, I've come to realize the profound essence of life's unpredictability and the importance of cherishing every moment. His departure has left an indelible mark, reminding me of the fragility of human existence and the inevitability of change.

Through the pain of loss, I've found solace in the memories we created together and the wisdom he imparted. I carry his spirit of resilience, love, and compassion as I navigate my path. May his legacy inspire me to embrace life's challenges gracefully and cherish the bonds that truly matter.

In honouring his memory, I commit to living each day with gratitude, humility, and a renewed sense of purpose. For in the tapestry of life, his presence remains woven into the fabric of my being, guiding me toward a future imbued with hope and resilience.

In "The Hidden Radiance: Unveiling the Untold Saga of a Quiet YOIGI embark on a spiritual journey to uncover the profound and often overlooked dimensions of a truly remarkable yet enigmatic sage. This narrative delves into the life of a silent guide whose name may not resonate with the masses but whose spiritual illumination has subtly shaped the paths of those in search of deeper truths. As the saga unfolds, it reveals not only the sage's extraordinary wisdom but also the trials and divine revelations that moulded his sacred quest. Through this journey, readers will uncover the hidden radiance that transcends mere recognition, discovering a timeless source of inspiration and spiritual enlightenment that whispers through the ages. This book offers a deep spiritual exploration, inviting readers to embrace the luminous wisdom concealed beneath the surface and to reflect on the quiet yet powerful forces that guide our souls.

Karunamayi Amma: A Beacon of Divine Motherhood

Born as Venkata Lakshmi in the serene village of Agraharam, she exemplified a rare blend of patience, compassion, and spiritual fortitude. Her life journey, marked by early challenges and profound spiritual encounters, illuminated the path of her maternal devotion. From overcoming health adversities to nurturing her family with boundless love and traditional wisdom, Karunamayi Amma's presence transcended ordinary motherhood. Her legacy, etched in acts of selfless kindness and unwavering faith, continues to inspire generations, embodying the timeless essence of maternal grace and spiritual resilience."

****

Excluding six children who reached heaven to make our entry onto Earth possible, we are four siblings to our parents. My mother, Venkata Lakshmi, is known for her patience and compassion. She never confined her love to her beloveds, but it encompassed whosoever she interacted with, including servant maids.

Divine Maternal Love

She used to adopt all the rituals for the sake of my father, Krishna Murthy, who was born Avadootha and has undergone lots of suffering throughout his life journey. She is beyond the framework of a normal, worldly woman. She hailed from Agraharam, a remote village in Bukkapatnam Mandal, Sri Sathya Sai District in Andhra Pradesh.

She is unique in her entire family circle and is never greedy. We can see contentment in her attitude, thinking, and actions. She married in May 1945, before reaching puberty, since there were child marriages in those days. It was a consanguine marriage, and my mother's father was the brother of my father's mother.

Despite enduring tuberculosis after her marriage and later undergoing a hysterectomy, she remarkably managed to evade major health complications. Amidst her challenges, she found solace in her deep spiritual connection. She recounted moments when she perceived the presence of her beloved deity, Raghavendra, envisioning him with his divine *KAMADALAM* and imparting sacred *MANTRASHITULU*. Furthermore, during a severe illness requiring hospitalization in Bangalore, she experienced a profound encounter with Sri Calluru Venkatanarayana Swamy, a mystic saint of Tadakaleru Ashram.

These spiritual encounters gave her strength and illuminated her path with hope and healing during her distress. Her patience has been exceptional, even in disasters at all phases of her life. She never used to talk loudly and used to feel very inconvenient if someone in the family shouted or talked loudly. She never used to answer if someone, including her children or husband, created a situation she disliked.

An Emblem of Tranquility and Grace

She is an expert cook, and we hardly purchased outside food, for she used to prepare nice dishes, including common snacks found in most traditional Brahmin families. For a period, I thought that I was the first child of my parents, and she never shared the tragedy of losing her five precious children before we were born.

She faced lots of trouble in staying with her in-laws and withstood testing periods, including her life-threatening health issues, even during periods of immobility and the passing of her husband and dearest daughter to the heavenly world. Her expression of unbearable bruised feelings due to unmanageable situations reflected in her tears pierced my heart. Her lips shone pink, and her captivating smile and fully covered dress always make us feel she is something unique with divine qualities.

She richly deserves the name KARUNAMAYI, for her kindness knows no bounds. She embodies tranquillity with lips as pink as petals and a face graced with elegance. Her eyes, peaceful and serene, reflect a heart overflowing with compassion. With ears attuned to the whispers of empathy, she listens with unwavering patience.

Her nurturing spirit shines through in her gentle words and soothing conversations. Her culinary creations are a testament to her untiring efforts, leaving mouths watering with delight. Never does she raise her voice, yet her presence speaks volumes of tolerance and grace: Behold, KARUNAMAYI AMMA, a beacon of kindness and a symbol of unwavering love.

Spiritual Teachings and Guiding Light

She knew about us and never intruded by asking personal questions like jobs or settling into life by marriage. She never entertained any worldly talk. My memories with my mother, a divine incarnate, are beyond expression and should be confined to myself since it dilutes the power of her soul. My brother Hari's Telugu Album on Mother is a true reflection of his feelings for her, who is no less than a wonderful "Universal Mother".

She found solace in meditating upon her TALI BOTTU. The sacred thread tied by her spouse during their marriage held deep sentimental value for her. Since childhood, she cherished wearing a nose thread, a symbol of enduring traditions.

Her guidance to us was firm: after our father's passing, she insisted we refrain from tonsuring, believing it could jeopardize her well-being. We honoured her wishes, prioritizing her happiness over societal expectations.

Society often criticized but rarely supported us, focused more on pinpointing our choices rather than sharing our joys or comforting our sorrows, unlike the community of like-minded individuals we cultivated. What came from our mother's mouth was considered VEDA, for she spoke with sincerity, and her words were

balanced in heart, thought, and action.

She was not merely an earthly mother but a mother who embraced the world of goodness. Our joy stemmed from nurturing our intimate circle rather than seeking validation from the superficial norms of the world.

My mother never removed her ornaments, even after the demise of her spouse. She asked us to throw saris given by relatives as part of a ritual after my father's demise. She said that saris were given without jackets since it was not auspicious. *'Till yesterday, giving anything to me was auspicious. Just because your father is not in the physical body, they provide only a sari as it was a ritual observed by all in society".*

She used to say that a ritual performed only on the day of demise was to remember beloveds only on that day, whether out of love or fear, and for those who are an integral part of their soul, observing rituals makes no sense. *'The only ritual which you should all observe is to be good at all times, causing no harm to others and yourself, and lead a pure life devoid of remark, praise or criticism".* In fact, of our two eyes, one my mother and sister, and the other one our beloved Father. We used to see the world by keeping them as our lens.

A Tribute to Divine Motherhood

My inability to treat mothers and prevent specialist doctors from prescribing the wrong medication in higher doses, and the aftermath consequences, making my mother immobile and increasing her dependency on service maids who virtually harassed her physically and mentally, have strong imprints in my mind. She is great; she could bear such unbearable things with a smiling face. A teardrop from their eyes is an indication of her suffering, both physical and psychological, but she never used to say about it. Even in higher temperatures, she used to help my father in pooja (workshop), prepare food for us, and fall asleep after taxing her body.

In her tender words to our brother, Hari, referring to him as "Haripriya," our mother delicately weaves a tapestry of love and loss. This endearing nickname not only reflects her deep affection but also signifies her attempt to heal the void left by the passing of our dear sister. By explaining that he is both her son and daughter, she reveals a heartfelt longing to nurture and embrace familial bonds despite enduring profound grief. This dual role embodies her resilience and the enduring strength of maternal love, capturing the intricate emotions of longing, love, and loss within her maternal heart.

My brother, Dr Hari, used to serve her coffee while confined to bed, and she played nicely with him, pretending she was sleeping. My brother knew about it and used to call it Amma, Amma, Get up. Later, she used to get up with a smile when he held her hand tightly. The first word she used to utter was, 'Thanks APPA'. She repeated this almost daily for all she received from us, be it coffee, Tiffin, or medicine. We used to feel sorry for not saying thanks to Mother when she used to serve. We used to take everything for granted. The value of persons is realized only in their absence; that is the power of Maya.

Wisdom and Continuity

She is fond of mangoes and jackfruits. When we shifted to a new house, my father and mother sowed the mango seeds after eating the pulp. Today, both trees, representing our parents, have grown, giving us hundreds of mangoes. The tree planted by my mother is not for pickles but only for eating. Its colour is pinkish and very tasty, while the one planted by my Father is excellent for pickles.

My mother is an expert in making different types of mango pickles, and my father used to assist my mother. Like SHIVA PARVATHI, both served their children with divine love and extended the same with others with much more profundity.

Navigating Life's Challenges with Profound Sensitivity

I have grappled with an extraordinary level of sensitivity throughout my life. This trait transcends mere physical discomfort and delves into a realm where everyday occurrences evoke intense sensations akin to physical assault. The sound of mango branches being ruthlessly struck, for instance, would trigger debilitating headaches, as if my head were being mercilessly hammered. Similarly, the sight of cloth being torn before me felt like a piercing assault on my being.

My sensitivity extends beyond the physical realm; even mundane tasks, such as administering injections to my ailing mother, become excruciatingly painful experiences. Witnessing her illness compounded the agony, amplifying the emotional toll of my hypersensitivity.

Despite attempts to rationalize or mitigate this sensitivity, I've accepted it as an inherent aspect of my being, possibly inherited from past lives. While nature or a higher power may have ordained this predisposition, grappling with its implications has often left me in despair.

Yet, amidst the struggle, there lies a glimmer of resilience. Through introspection and acceptance, I endeavour to navigate life's challenges with grace, recognizing that my sensitivity, though burdensome, is also a testament to the depth of my empathy and connection to the world around me.

The Legacy Lives On

With the departure of her soul from her physical body on the auspicious day of Varalakshmi, my life plunged into a deep well of depression. It felt as though an essential part of my being—mind, body, and spirit—had been brutally torn away by the relentless hand of fate. My younger brother bore witness to a phenomenon: a light that seemed to traverse from our home to the towering Gopuram of the temple of the Lord of Seven Hills, a few yards away.

Amid my grief, I realized the profound lessons my mother's life and passing had imparted. Her unwavering love, boundless compassion, and selfless sacrifices were not merely acts of maternal duty but manifestations of divine grace. She taught us the value of humility, patience, and kindness, guiding us toward righteousness and spiritual growth.

As I reflect on her legacy, I understand that the true essence of her being transcends the physical realm. Her spirit lives on in the bond of love that connects us, her children, to the divine essence of the universe. Through her example, she instilled in us the importance of cherishing every moment, expressing gratitude for the blessings bestowed upon us, and embracing the interconnectedness of all beings.

Though her physical presence may no longer grace our lives, her spirit continues illuminating our journey, guiding us with the light of her love. In honouring her memory, we honour the sacred bond between mother and child, recognizing it as a timeless expression of divine love and grace.

A Mother's Eternal Love: A Beacon Beyond Life

In those final moments, as my brother Hari sat beside *our mother*, his heart was heavy with helplessness and disbelief. He gently said, "Amma, I'm praying for you."

With the grace and wisdom only a mother possesses, she replied softly, "There is no need. Spending time with me is more important. You've been holding back, not giving me permission to leave, even though your sister and father have been calling me. I've stayed all these years, enduring pain because I couldn't bear to leave you without a mother. But now, it's time. I don't want to burden you any longer."

Her words, filled with love and peace, struck Hari deeply. Overwhelmed with emotion, he laid his head on her heart, and immediately, a gentle sound resonated. She started playing with his hair and lips, the way she had done when he was a child. At that moment, Hari became a little boy again, forgetting his age, the world around him, and even his worries. He felt the pure warmth of her touch as if time had folded back to those precious years.

Later that night, she called for him again. "Hari, you need to sleep with me tonight. Who will attend to me when I call? The servant maid will be in deep sleep. I cannot ask Nagaraj to stay awake; though he's older, he's still a child, and of course, he is God. Ganesh is far away in Bangalore. Vasantha left three years ago, and your father followed soon after. Who can I call? Who will help me? You are the only one I have left, and that's why I look for you."

With deep care, Hari replied, "Amma, I'm just in the next room. Call me, and I'll be with you in seconds."

She smiled gently, knowing more than she let on. "Alright, but come when I call once. I cannot repeat it. Tonight, I will disturb you."

As predicted, she called him around midnight, between 2:30 and 3:00 AM. Hari rushed to her side within seconds and saw her struggling for breath. He immediately called me, but by the time we both reached her, holding her in our arms, *our mother* took her last breath.

In that sacred moment, she conquered death. Her face glowed with a peaceful radiance we had never seen before. There was a divine smile on her lips as though she had found her final rest, ready to reunite with the ones who had called her home.

In my anguish, I broke down. I shouted angrily at the Gods. How could they take someone so precious from us? In my innocence and desperation, I questioned Baba. A mother is irreplaceable, and although I knew life's journey was not eternal, I could not accept losing her.

What we feared most was not just her physical absence but the loss of her love, nurturing care, and divine guidance. Yet, deep within, I knew the truth—God has His plans, and no matter how deeply we are attached, He executes them silently and perfectly. He is the Director of life's play, and we are the actors following His script.

Our mother had stayed with us, enduring her pain for our sake. But now, her time had come. Though heartbreaking, she had played her role with grace and sacrifice, and her departure was part of the divine plan. What we miss most isn't her physical presence but the love and light she brought into our lives.

Her love is eternal, transcending even death. Though she is no longer with us in body, her spirit, wisdom, and guidance will forever remain in our hearts, like a beacon of light in the dark moments of life.

We were both alone, silently gazing at each other, with the memory of our dear mother weighing heavy on our hearts, tears streaming down our faces, flowing without end. My brother, Dr. Hari, a talented lyricist, poured his soul into creating nine beautiful Telugu songs in the Amma Telugu Album (2013), available on YouTube, released by Aditya Musicals. Every word and note were his own—written, tuned, but sung by leading singers with devotion. He used to lay beside our mother, patting her gently as one would comfort a child, finding in those moments an indescribable, blissful connection.

When I asked him why he chose to compose nine songs, his answer resonated deeply. "For nine months, a child is cradled in the mother's womb, cherished and nurtured without a single complaint. The number nine symbolizes not only this sacred bond but also the nine forms of devotion and the nine planetary forces that find solace when we seek the blessings of Mother Shakti." These songs were not merely a gift to our mother—they were a profound expression of our love and gratitude.

One particular song, laden with the weight of her sacrifices and struggles, moved her deeply. As its melody filled the room, her tears flowed freely, reflecting our own silent sorrow. They were tears of shared grief and heartfelt remembrance, ones we could not console but felt profoundly.

Today, my brothers and I bow in reverence to the millions of mothers around the world. May their blessings cleanse our minds, and may their love continue to purify our hearts.

Our heartfelt appeal to sons and daughters is this: "Pursue success through hard work—there is no fault in seeking prosperity. Yet, let us not forsake our parents in the process. They are living manifestations of the divine who gave us life and nurtured us with unwavering love. Our accomplishments, intelligence, and positions in life are the fruits of their selfless sacrifices. Neglecting them is disconnecting from our essence, the divine, and the world surrounding us.

In today's fast-paced world, where materialism often overshadows spiritual values, let us not be consumed by greed. We can strive for success while remaining mindful of our true needs, not letting the pursuit of wealth drown us in a sea of sorrow. This message serves as a gentle reminder of our spiritual duty to our parents, who, in their twilight years, seek the love and care they once gave so freely. Their longing for affection is not just a plea for comfort but a call to recognize our sacred bond. By honouring and supporting them, we fulfil our spiritual responsibilities and embrace the values of compassion, gratitude, and reverence that are the true essence of our existence.

Our Mother, Our Teacher

Despite only having a primary education, our mother imparted invaluable life lessons through her subtle interactions and guidance. Her wisdom shaped us profoundly, guiding us beyond mere words. Here are some of her key teachings:

1. **Guard Your Personal Information:** *Avoid sharing your age with those whose intentions or demeanour seem harmful.*

   Rationale: Sharing personal details with individuals who may have negative intentions can expose you to unnecessary risks. Spiritually, maintaining discretion protects your personal energy and ensures you are surrounded by those who respect your privacy. For example, if someone exhibits a critical or invasive attitude, it's wise to keep personal information private to safeguard your well-being.

2. **Avoid Over-Praising:** *While acknowledging achievements is important, excessive praise can lead to unintended consequences, such as creating pressure and unrealistic expectations.*

   Rationale: Over-praising can increase stress and anxiety, disrupting inner peace and spiritual balance.

Offering constructive feedback rather than excessive praise supports personal growth and maintains spiritual equanimity. For example, rather than showering someone with praise for every minor success, provide balanced feedback that fosters self-improvement and maintains realistic expectations.

3. **Practice Rituals Wisely:** *Follow traditions and rituals as long as they don't burden you physically, economically, or emotionally.*

   Rationale: Rituals should enhance your spiritual practice without causing stress or discomfort. Spirituality thrives when practices are meaningful and manageable, not burdensome. For instance, participating in religious ceremonies should uplift you spiritually, not deplete your energy or resources.

4. **Be Cautious with Forecasters:** *Don't reveal your hands to astrologers or palm readers, as they are often uncertain about their own futures and may not offer accurate insights about yours.*

   Rationale: Relying on external predictions can lead you away from trusting your own spiritual insights and judgment. True spiritual guidance comes from within, and external forecasters may not provide the clarity you seek. Trust in your own intuitive understanding and spiritual wisdom.

5. **Control Your Reactions:** *Don't shout or lose your temper, especially in the presence of others. It drains your energy and can lead to later feelings of guilt.*

Rationale: Maintaining composure helps preserve your spiritual energy and fosters inner peace. Reacting with anger or frustration can disturb your spiritual balance and lead to regrets. For example, staying calm in tense situations helps maintain harmony and protects your spiritual well-being.

6. **Be Devotional, Not Emotional:** *Cultivate devotion without letting emotions cloud your spiritual practices.*

   Rationale: True devotion arises from a place of spiritual clarity rather than emotional turbulence. Focus on your spiritual practices with a sense of calm and purpose rather than letting personal emotions dictate them. This approach ensures a deeper and more authentic connection to your spiritual path.

7. **Self-Reliance is Key:** *Don't always rely on others for help; take initiative and avoid waiting passively.*

   Rationale: Spiritual growth involves self-reliance and proactive engagement in your journey. Dependence on others for support can hinder your personal and spiritual development. Embrace self-sufficiency and take responsibility for your own growth and actions.

8. **Action Over Words:** *Follow through on your intentions with prompt action rather than merely talking about what you will do.*

   Rationale: Effective spiritual practice requires action that aligns with your intentions. Words alone are insufficient without corresponding actions. Demonstrating your commitment through concrete steps reinforces your spiritual goals and creates meaningful progress.

9. **Respectful Observations:** *When interacting with women, see them with respect and understanding, as you would view your own family members.*

   Rationale: Treating others with respect and empathy reflects your spiritual values and fosters harmonious relationships. Viewing others through the lens of respect and understanding enhances your spiritual interactions and builds positive connections.

10. **Mind Your Words:** *Think carefully before speaking to avoid later regrets. Control your tongue and choose your words thoughtfully.*

    Rationale: Words have a profound impact on relationships and spiritual harmony. Speaking thoughtfully ensures that your words reflect your true intentions and maintain spiritual integrity. For example, pausing to consider your response before speaking can prevent misunderstandings and preserve harmony.

11. **Prioritize Serving Those in Need:** *Direct your efforts toward helping individuals who are genuinely in need of assistance rather than focusing on those who no longer require your support.*

Rationale: Serving those who are in genuine need reflects the highest spiritual values of compassion, empathy, and selflessness. By channelling your energy and resources toward those who truly benefit from your assistance, you align with the deeper purpose of service and meaningful impact. This approach honours the spiritual principle of giving selflessly, nurturing the soul, and fulfilling a higher calling. It fosters a sense of purpose and connection, as you contribute to the well-being of others and create positive ripples in the global spiritual world cut across all religions, ideologies and philosophies.

12. **Simplicity Brings Clarity:** *A complex mind leads to confusion, while a simple heart fosters spiritual growth and clarity.*

    Rationale: Spiritual clarity often comes from simplicity and focus. Simplifying your approach to life and problems helps clear your mental clutter and fosters a deeper connection to your spiritual path. For example, breaking down complex issues into manageable parts can lead to greater understanding and spiritual insight.

13. **Generosity in Relationships:** *Maintain relationships by being a giver rather than a receiver. Avoid acting like a beggar when you have much to offer.*

    Rationale: Generosity enriches relationships and aligns with spiritual principles of selflessness. By giving freely and avoiding the mindset of neediness, you contribute positively to relationships and reflect spiritual abundance. Offer support and kindness without expecting immediate returns.

14. **Give Love Freely:** *Show pure love to others without expecting it in return, as diluted love can be painful to endure.*

    Rationale: Pure love, offered without conditions, embodies spiritual purity and deep compassion. When you expect something in return, it can diminish the true essence of your affection. By loving selflessly, you preserve the genuine nature of your emotions and avoid the disillusionment that can come from unmet expectations.

15. **Communicate with Empathy:** *Good communication, paired with empathy, ensures you are remembered positively. Poor communication or mere sympathy can tarnish your personality.*

    Rationale: Effective communication that includes empathy strengthens relationships and enhances spiritual connection. Empathetic interactions build positive impressions and foster understanding, while a lack of empathy can harm your relationships and personal reputation.

16. **Equitable Service:** *In today's society, it is crucial for sons to serve their parents with the same dedication and care as daughters do. While daughters often remember and attend to their parents' needs with deep understanding, there is a concerning trend where some sons may neglect*

their parental duties, leading to situations such as placing parents in old age homes.

Rationale: Equitable service within the family reflects the values of fairness, respect, and shared responsibility. Daughters often exhibit a profound commitment to their parents' well-being, understanding their needs and expectations. Sons should mirror this level of care and dedication, recognizing that parental support is a mutual responsibility. This approach aligns with spiritual principles of justice and compassion, emphasizing that every family member, regardless of gender, should contribute to the welfare of their parents. By adopting this balanced and respectful approach, we honour our parents and foster a culture of empathy and equity that can positively influence societal norms and family dynamics.

17. **Hold back your Tears:** *When possible, try to hold back your tears, as you may find clarity and answers later.*

    Rationale: Managing your emotional responses allows you to maintain spiritual focus and find solutions over time. Holding back tears can lead to greater emotional clarity and understanding, enhancing your spiritual journey and problem-solving abilities.

18. **Exercise Patience:** *When others are unresponsive or slow to react, remain patient. Losing patience can make it difficult to recover and maintain your composure.*

Rationale: Patience aligns with spiritual principles of tolerance and acceptance. Maintaining composure despite delays or unresponsiveness helps preserve your inner peace and relationships, reflecting spiritual maturity and resilience.

In essence, our mother's teachings reflect profound wisdom and practical guidance for life. Though challenges may arise, a mother's love and dedication remain unwavering. Cherish and worship mothers, for their guidance is invaluable, their blessings are boundless, and their love is a true source of strength and inspiration.

Spiritual Resilience: Navigating Adversity with Faith and Family Bonds

Prosperity to Poverty

My father, Krishna Murthy, hailed originally from Dharmavaram. His father, a revered priest, meticulously crafted the Telugu Panchangam, a sacred Hindu Calendar (Almanac). They were blessed with landed property, but their peace was disrupted when a relative of my grandfather, or someone similarly connected, laid claim to the land. The ensuing legal battle stripped them of much of their inheritance, plunging them into the depths of poverty. This journey from prosperity to poverty was not just a tale of loss but a testament to the family's unwavering spiritual resilience. This strength guided them through the darkest of times.

Family Struggles and Losses

My father's brother, a stamp vendor by trade, delved deeply into the mystical realms of astrology. He fulfilled the priest's marriage duties and presided over other auspicious ceremonies, such as housewarming rituals.

Another younger brother of my father, a promising doctor, tragically succumbed to leukaemia at a tender age. The loss of this radiant soul, whose beauty emanated tranquillity, left a void that could never be filled. Amidst these familial struggles and losses, spirituality remained a guiding light, providing solace and understanding.

Adoption and Family Bonds

At the tender age of seven or eight, my father was transplanted into the warmth of Achamma's embrace, leaving behind the woman who birthed him. Yet, it seemed destined that he was the missing piece of her heart. Their bond blossomed, infusing her life with unbridled joy, and she fiercely embraced her adopted son, her love tinged with possessiveness. This adoption was not only a physical act but a spiritual union that transcended blood ties.

Challenges and Triumphs in Adulthood: Navigating Tragedy with Grace

My grandmother's story embodies the profound ups and downs of life's journey. Despite her captivating beauty, she was thrust into widowhood at a tender age, forced to endure the stringent rituals of Brahminical tradition that stripped away her identity, from the shaving of her head to the removal of her bangles. While these customs carried deep cultural significance, they bore the weight of oppression, sparking societal resistance and reluctant acceptance. Yet, amidst these trials, spirituality emerged as a steadfast source of resilience and purpose for my grandmother.

Honesty and Hard Work

After marriage, my father moved to Andhra Pradesh after the Bifurcation of States. He was allotted to the irrigation department and shifted from the Sales Tax Department in Bellary. He worked as a clerk in different places, including Rayadurg, Kanekal, Penakacherla, BT Project, Mylavaram, and at the end of his service at Anantapur. Despite the trials of his career, spirituality guided my father's actions, anchoring him in honesty and integrity.

Transition into Retirement

We were born late, but how my father managed to run his family is known to both my parents. My mother wept on the day of his retirement and shed tears in Raghavendra Swamy Temple. One finds the idol of Sri Sathya Narayana Swamy in the same temple; my mother is a strong devotee of both deities and prayed to them to fetch an amount to feed her children and maintain her family. In this transition into retirement, spirituality became a source of strength and resilience for my family.

The Harmony of Devotion and Wisdom

1. From Work to Deepened Worship

After retiring from his job, my father's commitment to worship deepened, marking a profound shift in his life. For him, work had always been a form of worship, but with retirement, his devotion to prayer intensified significantly. What were once brief daily rituals transformed into hours-long sessions of deep spiritual communion?

He would spend extended periods in the prayer hall, often from 11 a.m. until well after 2:30 p.m., and sometimes even until 3 p.m., entirely absorbed in his connection with the divine. His worship, especially with the fragrant night jasmine, became more than a ritual—it became a sacred journey where he lost himself in the presence of the divine, so much so that he would forget about his meals and the passage of time. This heightened spirituality became the cornerstone of his post-retirement life, filling him with immense joy, peace, and a renewed sense of purpose.

2. Master of Yogic Practices

My father's devotion extended beyond traditional worship to include a mastery of yogic practices he had learned during his college days. He was particularly skilled in rotating his stomach like a ball and was an expert in *Dhauti Kriya*, a cleansing practice that purifies the oesophagus and stomach. This rigorous routine involved drinking warm saline water, swallowing and regurgitating cloth, and thoroughly cleansing the mouth, throat, and stomach. These practices were not just about maintaining physical health—they were a way to align his body, mind, and spirit, preparing him for deeper spiritual experiences.

3. A Seamless Transition Between Tasks One of the most remarkable aspects of my father was his ability

to switch seamlessly between different tasks, always maintaining a sense of balance and detachment. Whether he was meditating, watching a 20-over cricket match on television, listening to music, collecting flowers for prayer, or cooking food, he approached each activity with the same level of dedication and excellence. This ability to remain fully engaged yet inwardly detached was a secret to his good health and contentment. He taught us that being present in every moment, without being overly attached, was key to living a fulfilling life.

4. **Boundless Love and Compassion** My father's love for his family extended beyond his immediate relatives. He loved his brothers and sisters even more than his own children and treated everyone who came to our home with the same warmth and care. He never discriminated between his own family and others, embodying a spirit of inclusiveness and equality. Caste and social status meant nothing to him—he treated everyone as his own, moving effortlessly among people from all walks of life with the same love and respect.

5. **From Rituals to Rationalism** After his intense prayer sessions, my father would shift from being a devout ritualist to a rational thinker. He strongly advised us against consulting palmists or astrologers, believing that life is a divine plan set by God, with no shortcuts to solving problems. He often reminded us that everyone faces challenges, but these difficulties become easier to manage when we approach them with calmness and faith. He

believed that when we take problems in stride, we can feel the invisible hands of God extending help when we need it most.

6. **Reverence for Food and Life** My father's spirituality also manifested in his deep respect for food. Having experienced poverty in childhood, he never wasted even a single grain, often reminding us that God resides in every grain of food. To throw food away was, in his eyes, to discard the divine. He always advised us to serve food even to an enemy who approached with hunger, believing that we were honouring God in feeding others. His life was a celebration of God's design, and he never once uttered the word "boredom." To him, every moment was an opportunity to connect with the divine and live with purpose.

7. **A Life of Purpose and Peace** Through his unwavering devotion, mastery of yogic practices, and rational approach to life, my father taught us invaluable lessons about the meaning of life. His deep spirituality, combined with his love for others and his respect for all aspects of life, created a life of purpose and peace. He showed us that true devotion is not just about rituals but about living each moment with mindfulness, compassion, and an unshakable faith in the divine plan.

Unique Incidents and Inner Strength

I recall one rare, amazing thing that happened. My brother called the Horticulture Officer, who also brought his assistant. My father was in the prayer room and observed our conversation regarding the SAPOTA tree, which was very big with widened branches but did not yield any fruit. The horticulture assistant told my brother that the tree was neither male nor female, and it was a neutral gender and would never yield any fruit.

He suggested I cut it off and plant a new one. My father overheard it and, with a piercing look, shouted at them, stating, if you cut the tree or cause harm to it, I will not enter the house and leave it then and there itself. My brother asked him to be cool and told him he would never allow such things to happen.

Later, my father told him that the plant he carried gave shade and was enough. To our wonder, within one or two months, we noticed flowering, and it started yielding PALA SAPOTA of amazing size and taste. I realized that trees speak and have feelings, but we are too poor to understand their language and feelings. I resembled my father because plucking even a leaf used to cause me lots of pain, too. This incident was a testament to my father's deep spiritual connection with nature, demonstrating his inner strength and conviction.

Legacy and Lasting Impressions

Whatever he does, whether washing clothes or vegetables, ironing or cutting vegetables, or preparing any food item, he is unique and maintains consistency. His switchover of tasks within a fraction of a second is ample evidence of calling him a great Avadootha. He has a great interest in farming and used to invest more than what he was getting. He used to ask me to pay Rs.50 or Rs.100 and go to the post office to deposit, and he told us that money saved once would be helpful when we were in any crisis.

Any discussion, even for fun sake, about the sale of land since he was incurring loss due to the failure of rains, he used to get irritated. My brother used to tell my father that we would never dispose of lands to make money out of. We are the custodians of the lands and should never act against our parents' wishes, which is like God's mandate. Spirituality permeated every aspect of my father's life, guiding his actions and leaving a lasting impression on all who knew him.

Grieving Losses and Finding Purpose

He shed tears when his dearest daughter left him to reach the abode of peace in Heaven. He used to gaze at Baba seriously on certain occasions when situations became unmanageable, and his psychic association with Baba or other incarnations could not be comprehended. He imparted profound wisdom to us, cautioning against following his path as a clerk, for society often casts a disparaging glance upon such roles. Instead, he urged us to seek enlightenment through education and pursue vocations that uplift our souls and stature. The loss of his daughter deepened his spiritual resolve, guiding him to find purpose amidst grief.

Guidance and Reflections

With great reverence, my father advised my brother, Dr Hari, who now holds the esteemed position of Director at RDT, to remain steadfast despite tempting offers from renowned institutions and prestigious projects. He had all gratitude for Father Vincent Ferrer, for he recognized my brother's knowledge and skill, which were dormant for many years.

I, too, believe that contentment gives peace, and peace prevails when we realize that God gives us what is suitable to us rather than what we richly or meritoriously deserve. To my father, those who recognize and nurture our talents are akin to divine emissaries sent by a benevolent universe. He believed that their patronage was akin to spiritual sustenance, far surpassing the material rewards offered by those who only acknowledge our worth after it has been proven through experience. His guidance was practical and deeply spiritual, urging us to seek fulfilment beyond worldly success.

Final Farewell and Legacy

The helpless situation of my mother being confined to bed and my sister leaving her physical body created a big void. He suddenly fell sick, and local doctors suggested shifting him to Bangalore for higher institutions. I knew the outcome of super specialty hospitals, and the same thing happened again. I was helpless, and God tightened my hand to intervene. It may seem puzzling to others, but I knew how I suffered. It is like asking for Water, standing next to the Ganges with the hands tightened. Such a situation should never come to any doctor. I regret that God should have made me a beggar, not a doctor who is useless to society or my family.

Recalling my sister

I feel like recalling my sister here. I have only one sister, Vasantha Lakshmi, and I named her SAI NIVEDITHA. She did her postgraduation in Geography and later obtained a Master's and Doctorate of Philosophy in the same subject, apart from her Bachelor's Degree

in Education, to pursue a teaching profession. She worked as a postgraduate teacher in one of the private schools offering a CBSE syllabus. She studied at Sathya College until Graduation and is an adorer of Sri Sathya Sai Baba.

She used to worship 'SANTOSHIMATA' for our health and well-being. Her dress was decent and an icon of purity and divine virtue. Her services towards her brothers defy any definition. She used to wash our clothes, including our underwear, and such a sister is a rare boon to us. She never liked marriage and intended to settle down at Tiruvannamalai. She was fascinated by Bhagwan Ramana Maharshi.

There was pressure on our parents to perform her marriage since all of us were unmarried due to God's Choice. As a lady, her views were not considered, and my parents settled her marriage with a guy based in Hyderabad. As I wouldn't say I liked the whole matrimony process, I left for Kasapuam on the day they came to see and settle the alliance. They posed several restrictions, like she should not do any job, should be confined to four walls, and many silly ones.

Fall of Jasmine Flower into Fire

My brother, Dr Hari, took the whole burden, including convincing her and extending support to my parents to perform her marriage, which proved a big mirage. She suffered a series of problems, both physical and psychological, and was confined to a pyre at the end. I feel that we failed, as brothers, to give her solace when needed because our attention was polarized on our aged parents, and our professional obligations rendered her helpless during acute sickness. She virtually fought her disease with ease but decided to leave this world to go back to the place from where she came to serve us. Certain incarnations take birth for reasons unknown to us, and they appear and disappear like lightning during rains. She is one such special person in our lives whose aura used to magnify our existence, and with her departure, we faced a big void in our lives.

We lately realized that Gender discrimination prevails well within most families, and we hardly care about listening to girls' feelings and choices and letting them alone to make decisions that appease their souls. We are bothered by the society around us, which hardly understands us and is ever ready to find faults in us and aspire to our downfall by all means. We should create a society of our own where like-minded people connected to our soul only exist, and the rest are need-based relationships that owe colourful shades that get shaded over a while.

She is courageous enough to face the hard realities of life. Her life is like that of a camphor pill or a candlelight. We felt we had thrown smiling jasmine into the fire as an offering to God. God alone knows how my brother, Dr Hari, faced acrimonious situations, and I rendered no help because of my bondage with my little sister and my feeling of separation. However, I met her and my parents in the Astral world one day.

My life darkened, and it became pale and dull after three persons who were connected to me from previous lives left me, leaving pain in my wounded heart. Although I tried to divert attention towards my teaching, it abruptly ended, and I realized God wanted to make a Beggar. However, I owned a richness of wisdom that was enclosed and inoperative.

Before my Father left his physical body, he spoke to my brother, Hari, stating, "*I have seen SRI RAM, and I have shared my life road with him from the day I was born till now. I wept for a while because, in the event of my passing body, it becomes a burden to you to lead the family. Take care of your Mother, who is from a great cult and is a great lady. She is born only to suffer. Never hurt her by any means. She is very sensitive, but she never expresses what she wants. Her mode of communication is mostly silence to avoid misunderstanding or quarrelsome atmosphere.*"

The demise of my father due to medical negligence is something that pains me a lot. It happened in the case of my mother and sister, too. Being a doctor, I was helpless, and the cosmic doctor and director made me helpless. God looks to me, sometimes cruel, and it is difficult to decipher his kindness in that situation. The departure of Avadootha Nanna caused a void unfilled, resulting in my mother becoming absolutely sick. He left his body in less than 45 days of the demise of our lovely sister.

A state of gloominess

The departure of my parents and my only Sister made me feel that I had no business in this world, but my binding was my two brothers. The sickness of my younger brother, Gasha, further caused deep annoyance, and umpteen number of times, in my prayers, I used to invoke my spirits, and I was crying out bitterly in late nights to take my life to save my brother. I did penance for months during COVID-19, praying for ADITYA, the SURYA Bhagwan, the giver of light and life. We could speak philosophy and spiritualize things, but certain bondages in life are pure and sacred, and we are one such. I, along with my parents and siblings, am one soul residing in six bodies. My life's purpose is to spend time with all of them, but it is like a short holiday.

"In life's fleeting journey, each moment spent with loved ones is akin to a precious holiday, where the brevity of time underscores the importance of cherishing every second. Like a passing breeze, these moments are transient yet profoundly meaningful, weaving a tapestry of memories that linger long after the journey's end. Embracing the impermanence

of time, we find solace in the beauty of connection, knowing that the richness of our experiences lies in the love shared and the memories created along the way."

Spirituality emerges as a guiding force throughout this narrative, infusing every aspect of the family's journey with resilience, understanding, and purpose. From the upheaval of prosperity to the depths of poverty, from the loss of loved ones to the challenges of daily life, spirituality remains a steadfast companion, offering solace and strength. Whether through rituals, devotion, or an intimate bond with nature, the family finds meaning, resilience, and a deep connection to something greater than themselves. Their story is a testament to the transformative power of spirituality, guiding them through adversity and leaving a lasting legacy of faith, compassion, and spiritual evolution.

Embracing the Mysteries of Birth and the Spiritual Connection with Serpent Wisdom

Mysterious Beginnings

I am the sixth child of my parents, and my entry into the world is mysterious. The first child of my parents, Srinivasulu, as per my parents, was born special. He was named after our KULA DAIVAM, the Lord of Seven Hills. He frequently quoted examples and stories from Ramayana and Mahabharata, and his expression of feelings and communication was not typical of a child of tender age. My mother told me that she experienced surprise and a deep sense of fear, for he behaved so maturely and even educated my grandma when she was harsh with my mother.

My mother approached a famous astrologer, Sri Krishna Sastry, a priest in my mother's village, Agraharam, near Bukkapatnam, the present Satya Sai District. He told my mother that the child was born special and advised her to take care of him "until he reached 7 or 8 years". If he crossed that period, he would become a monk or reach a high societal position. My brother was fond of IDLI, and my mother made them frequently as he enjoyed them.

One day, my grandma took him to the Bazar, and on that day, my mother had not prepared IDLI. This made my grandma buy them at a local hotel. Immediately after consuming IDLI, he became sick, and the doctor diagnosed it as Cholera, for which there was no cure at that time. He passed away on my mother's lap, a devastating blow for my divine parents.

As usual, my mother had to endure insults for losing her beloved child, and my father, out of sheer love for his son, became psychologically disturbed and left home without informing anyone. He was not seen for over two nights until someone found him at a nearby railway station and brought him back home. My mother faced tough times, being blamed for all the misfortunes in the home. Her only support was my mother's sister, Kamalamma Peddamma, who lived in Bellary. My mother silently endured the insults and humiliations in the family.

My mother's love was as boundless as it was mysterious. Though she lovingly prepared IDLIS for us, she never partook in the meal herself. The reason behind her refusal remained a silent ache buried within her heart. It wasn't until one day when my brother insisted that she eat despite her illness, that the floodgates of her sorrow opened. Through tearful eyes, she confided that the memory of her lost son haunted her, leaving her restless and unable to enjoy the simple pleasures of life.

She would recount how he appeared to her, a small child without clothes, gently urging her to buy him garments. This poignant revelation shed light on the depth of her maternal love, transcending comprehension boundaries. Despite her pain, she continued to nurture and care for us, embodying the essence of maternal sacrifice and resilience.

My mother exemplified motherhood's profound strength and tenderness in her silent suffering and unwavering devotion. Like countless other mothers, she carried the weight of her grief silently, yet her love remained a beacon of warmth and compassion in our lives. She was a great mother in every sense of the word.

Trials and Tragedies

Later, my mother conceived and delivered a female child, Lalitha, who was like a divine BALA Tripura. She was so cute, but she, too, died before her first anniversary. This was followed by another child, Ramudu, who my mother told me looked so cute, followed by three other children who died within months of their birth. My mother was grateful that she could bear these testing periods. All of this necessitated my entry into the world.

My mother experienced cobras crawling all over her body, causing her great fear. She shared this with her sister, who suggested she pray to Lord Subramanyam for a son. Upon the advice of Sri Krishna Sastry, my parents performed NAGA PRATISHTA at Vidurashwatha, a small village in the Gauribidanur Taluk, Chikkaballapur District, Karnataka.

Spiritual Awakening and Purpose

Vidurashwatha Temple is near the Karnataka–Andhra Pradesh border, about 5 km from Gauribidanur. This place and the temple significantly influenced the Indian independence movement. Vishnu, Brahma, and Maheshwara are worshipped in the Vidhura Ashwatha Narayana Swamy Temple or Vidurashwatha Temple. The temple is famous for Santana Nagendra Swamy Pooja, Kalasarpadosha Pooja, and Naga Dosha Pooja.

My parents believed that losing children at repeated intervals was due to KALASARPA DOSHA, and they carried out penance for a week in a ritualistic way. Later, my mother conceived and delivered me, and they named me NAGARAJ.

My mother told me that I was born in a Jatka Bandi (horse-drawn cart) while she was on her way to Missionary Hospital in Bellary. She shared that I opened my eyes while in the Jatka, and it was a normal delivery. After I was born, our family celebrated big, and they believed that the Serpent God, Subramanya Devara, bestowed his spirit on him in the form of NAGA RAJ, the King of Serpents.

Since childhood, I have had a peculiar fascination with seeing and playing with snakes. I never feared them; I associated my existence with those wonderful creatures. Snake symbolism and the spiritual process in India are deeply intertwined, as they are in every part of the world, because wherever people became aware, they naturally recognized snakes' sensitivity to a certain type of energy, to meditativeness.

Snakes are much better than certain humans who emit vengeance and envy. It is not that cunning type of animal. If someone tells me that they killed a serpent in their home or office, I experience physical and psychological discomfort. My association with snakes is an enigma to others, and I casually used to tell my parents and family members that I am from NAGA or SARPA LOKA.

There are subtler planes of various degrees in the universe. One such world is the Naga Loka, translated as the World of Snakes. We talk about this world because it connects with humankind on earth. Some beings from this world came to earth and assisted/guided humanity with superior wisdom while humanity was meditating to find the ultimate truth and still evolving into a substantial civilization.

Although born with intrinsic qualities of bravery, for reasons unknown, this NAGA RAJ had to lead a life of subtlety, contrary to the nature of the divine snake.

When I hear someone causing harm to any girl or innocent person, I feel like attacking. My intrinsic nature is to attack, but paradoxically, I am confined to a cage, which is horrifying, causing much annoyance.

My mother used to joke with my brother, Hari, that all those who died prematurely are like gems" and "salagrams", and those born later as pebbles. This phrase carries a deeper meaning beyond its surface humour. In traditional Hindu culture, "gems" and "salagrams" are highly revered symbols of divine blessings and spiritual significance. Gems are considered precious stones that symbolize purity, wisdom, and prosperity, while salagrams are sacred stones representing the presence of the divine, particularly Lord Vishnu.

By jokingly referring to the children who passed away as "gems" and "salagrams," our mother implies that they were extraordinary and spiritually blessed beings. This suggests that their brief lives were filled with a special divine purpose despite their premature departure from this world.

On the other hand, the children born later, likened to "pebbles," may symbolize the ordinary or mundane aspects of life. This juxtaposition highlights the mother's acceptance of life's unpredictability and her recognition of the preciousness of every soul, regardless of their earthly status.

Her saying things in a jovial passion reflects a perspective of spiritual acceptance and reverence for the mysteries of life and death, emphasizing the belief that every being, whether perceived as precious or ordinary, holds inherent value and purpose in the grand tapestry of existence.

The Wooden Horse: A Journey of Self-Discovery and Spiritual Awakening

Exploring the Depths of Childhood's Magic

In the innocent simplicity of childhood lies a profound journey of self-discovery, an odyssey that transcends the boundaries of time and space. Encircled by the warm embrace of familial love and captivated by the enchanting allure of childhood toys, the soul embarks upon a voyage of exploration and wonder.

The Wooden Horse of Childhood

Within the cherished memories of days long past, the wooden horse stands as a beacon of playful innocence—a tender gift from our father's loving hand. Amidst the boundless realm of childhood imagination, I, as the sixth born, discovered solace within the embrace of parental affection, enveloped in the tender echoes of lost siblings.

In the enchanting world of make-believe, where adventures unfold and dreams take flight, the wooden horse became not just a toy but a companion, a confidant. Its sturdy form provided a sanctuary where I could escape the complexities of growing up, finding refuge in the comforting presence of familial love.

Despite its steadfast and motionless nature, the wooden horse transcends mere physicality. It becomes an vessel, encapsulating our parents' enduring love and devotion. Its significance stretches beyond its wooden exterior, serving as a poignant reminder of the unbreakable bonds that unite us as a family. Through the years, it remains a cherished symbol of enduring affection, a testament to the profound connection that binds us together through the passage of time.

The Illusion of Movement

As the years unfolded, I realized the stagnation within my existence, akin to the static nature of the wooden horse. The allure of external beauty fades, revealing life's illusionary facade and the transient nature of worldly pursuits.

The Embrace of Mother's Love

In my mother's embrace, I find refuge from the chaos of worldly desires. Her nurturing presence transcends time, guiding my spirit through life's labyrinth. Mother, whom I lovingly call my mother as Karunamayi Amma, Mother of

Compassion, exemplifies unwavering devotion, nurturing my soul above all else.

The Spiritual Awakening

Amid life's illusions, a deeper truth emerges. The divine presence of the Lord of Seven Hills manifests, guiding me towards enlightenment. In the sanctuary of familial love, I unravel the threads of past lives woven into our shared existence. Father, known as Avadhootha Nanna, Immortal Father, is an icon of ripened wisdom. At the same time, siblings embody spiritual roles — Hari, my dearest brother, as Karma Yogi, my 'Graceful Sister' as Sai Nivedita, and my younger brother, Ganesh or Gasha, as Balayogi — enriching our familial bond with their presence.

Transcending Material Existence: Embracing Truth

In the journey of life, amidst the echoes of childhood memories and the embrace of familial love, lies the revelation of the soul's journey. Like a wooden horse in a world of illusions, we are called to transcend the confines of material existence and embrace the truth that lies within.

In the tender embrace of a mother's love and the divine presence that surrounds us, we find solace amidst the tumult of existence, journeying towards the realization of our true essence. Through it all, the depth of familial love has adorned existence with beauty, even when the world may perceive it as mundane or trivial.

Journey of the Soul: Unveiling the Divine Path

Early Education and Family Celebration

My education was in a remote village, VEPARALA, near MYLAVARAM Dam Site, Jammalamadugu, in YSR Kadapa District. I still remember the most pleasant days when I learned that I was one of the few district candidates who scored first division; for that matter, I am the only student from my High School. It was a big celebration in my family, and my father hired a cook to prepare sweets and distribute them to the staff of the Irrigation Department, where my father worked as a senior assistant.

Academic Choices and Challenges

Getting a seat in Government Junior College at Jammalamadugu was easy, as I got the first division. My father bought the application form and asked me to fill it out and submit it to the college, and he was on camp for two days in Anantapur.

I opted for MPC, but the real drama in my life started after my father returned from camp. He scolded me for opting for Mathematics, not sciences, for my father intended me to become a doctor as my father's younger brother, who was a doctor, died of leukaemia.

My father went to college and requested the Principal and admitted me into BiPC against my will. Somehow, I completed my intermediate with good marks, and I told my father I intended to join a B.Sc. in agriculture, and he okayed it unmindfully, changing his mindset.

I had to be with Nature, for I derive joy when I am in tune with it, which means communion with God. I got a seat in B.Sc., Ag., but I still need to submit a certificate that we own land, for I applied to mention that we own land. We own land in Gooty, but my father didn't obtain a certificate mentioning land ownership.

My admission was rejected, and I joined a general B.Sc. in Government Arts College, Anantapur. I initially stayed in a rented room with my friend Prasad. I still remember my brother, Hari, writing letters to me mentioning B.S.C. next to my name.

He used to mention that my brother was studying at Bata Shoe Company, and it was sheer innocence, not a changed mindset from the village to the district environment. After my graduation, I applied for post-graduation in Bio-sciences at SK University.

Paradoxically, my admission was denied despite my fair qualifications, as someone with connections to higher authorities in the university secured admission through unfair means.

Despite scoring significantly lower than me on the entrance examination, their unjust influence prevailed. This experience is a stark reminder that while one may uphold fairness and integrity, the world around us may not always reciprocate with honesty. It underscores the unfortunate reality that deceit lurks in unexpected corners, ready to deceive even the most earnest and deserving individuals.

Navigating Educational Hurdles

My father started insisting that I should apply for medicine since my demised cousin also studied medicine after his B.Sc., Not saying "No" to my father, I started my preparation by unmindfully buying a few entrance books. For two consecutive years, I missed getting a seat in medicine very narrowly.

God designs either failure or success. I became so frustrated with criticism from within and outside that I applied for post-graduation at SV University and was admitted into Psychology.

My father retired long ago, and sending me outside Anantapur was risky. Hari, my brother, got an economically backward certificate from the Tahsildar, which helped me join the university college in Tirupathi.

I developed a fascination for Psychology, and many thoughts used to flash, and I started realizing the association between Mind and Body, and the Spirit too. All my seniors and lecturers developed affection, and for the first time, I enjoyed my stay and studies at SV University Hostel.

The footsteps of Lord of Seven Hills were visible from the Hostel where I studied. It was a wonderful stay that rejuvenated my spirits and was taking asylum at the holy feet of my favourite God, Sri Venkateswara Swamy.

Divine Encounters: Journeys of Spiritual Awakening

I came for holidays and went to my mother's native place, Agraharam. On the very first day, I encountered unanticipated situations. I feared facing Nights, for a Saint robed in saffron dress, whose face was not visible. He took me out of bed and soon kept me at Kurnool, where I could see the KURNOOL Medical College Board. Immediately, he drops me back to my village. All these used to happen within a fraction of a second.

I clearly remembered the saint firmly holding my hands, and repeating the same event for one week sapped my energies. I was restless. I used to go to the caves of Narasimha Swamy in our village by climbing the unformed steps. I used to strongly hit my head on the holy stone in the cave.

I had Darshan of Lord Rama, Lord Hanuman, Mother Sita and Lakshmana Swamy. This happened a couple of times, and I was trying to catch hold of the beautiful God Rama, but they used to disappear in no time. I felt happy because I could see them with my own eyes, and I had never shared this golden event with anyone except my brother Hari when I realized that my time on this earth would soon end.

Certain spiritual experiences we encounter, as designed by Nature, should be kept to ourselves. They are not for publicity since people dilute speaking them lightly with animosity and may label such persons as Mad people.

They say such experiences as Illusion, but they hardly know they illuminate your soul. I am labelled Mad since I used to always be in a prayerful mood. One should be mad after God, not mad after materialistic things. Sharing intricate or subtle feelings with undeserving people is to be avoided as per God's dictum.

After a week, I asked myself, *'Nagaraj, why do you fear?* What is there to fear? Things happen per God's design, and you have no control over what happens. I used to adore Bhagwan Puttaparthi Sai Baba and go to his abode to have HIS Dharshan the next day. I used to walk several kilometres alone, holding a small bag on my shoulders. When I reached the Ashram, I was told that Bhagwan left for Brindavan Ashram in Bangalore.

Out of frustration, I started my journey back to my native place. While walking in contemplation, I noticed a car suddenly stop, and the shutters of the car opened. With a full smile on HIS face, I noticed Baba waved both his hands, blessed me, and left. All this happened in a split second. I realized that the saint who appeared in our native village was Bhagwan, Sri Sathya Sai Baba.

It was my first encounter with Baba, and I never experienced such a miracle in life physically, although he used to appear in my dreams occasionally. I then went to Sai Geetha, a saint born as an elephant, to serve Baba.

I didn't fear facing it, although its caretaker warned me not to approach it directly. To my wonder, it blessed me by kneeling affectionately and keeping its trunk on my head. It was a memorable incident, and I considered it a good omen to appear for the medical entrance examination.

I read Prof. Kasturi's saying about Sai Geetha, "*In an age when human values struggle to find their way into human hearts when man's bestial tendencies often prevail upon the latent good in him, it is Divinity's masterplan that showcases the dedicated life of an elephant modelling devotion in its real and complete sense. Indeed, it serves as a great lesson to humanity*". *The association of Sai Geetha with Baba is beyond human comprehension, and only a few can decipher the association in the true sense.*

Unexpected Turns

I appeared for the entrance examination at Tirupathi without revealing it to my parents or family. I came on vacation to Anantapur, and suddenly, I noticed the results of the medicine entrance examination. I didn't bring my hall ticket, but I remembered my hall ticket number. I saw my number in the selected list but wanted to cross-check it before confirming it with my parents.

I told my father I needed to go to Tirupathi without mentioning the purpose. They expected something positive but didn't question me. The next day, I came from Tirupathi, bringing the news of my selection for the entrance examination. My father was virtually in tears, for I could fulfil his small desire to see me as a doctor. It was a small gift I intended to give my father, although becoming a doctor differed from my dream.

Entrance into Medical School

From becoming a psychologist, I changed my desire to become a psychiatrist by becoming a doctor and pursuing post-graduation in Psychiatry. I left my M.Sc. course without completing it. I joined MBBS at Government Medical College, Kurnool, where my father's younger brother, Dr Somasundaram, worked as a doctor and a tutor in pathology.

Challenges and Miracles

My father asked me to inform my PEDDAPPA (Father's Elder brother) at Dharmavaram, and innocently, I went there to share the good news. But for them, it was bad news because they were unwilling to imagine me in the position of doctor. They scolded me and faced a very insulting atmosphere, which depressed me. The world appeared to be a place of complexities, and I felt that I slipped into this world by oversight against God's will.

Except for our house, none encouraged me to join medicine. Paradoxically within a week of getting a seat in Medicine, I got qualified for the post of Assistant Station Master, a clerk in the food corporation of India (FCI) and a clerk cum Typist in Sanjamala Junior College, Kurnool.

Everybody suggested going for a job and settling down since doing medicine at that age is undesirable. It is natural for them to suggest this because they were envious of me doing medicine and rejecting Government Jobs.

Of course, they expected me to settle down and lead the life of an earthly person, supporting my parents financially since he was retired and finding it hard to educate my brothers and sister. My father didn't agree with their proposals, and he motivated me to join medicine, and I obeyed his instructions.

Divine Revelations: Guidance from Srinivasa Swamy

I met a born saint with whom I travelled in a couple of my previous births. He is Srinivasa Swamy, who is said to be the incarnation of Lord of Seven Hills. I had my spiritual encounters and many miracles, which I narrate separately. He used to stay in his Ashram at Jammalamadugu, and I thought of getting his blessings before joining Medicine.

The moment I shared the news, HE, with a surprising gesture, told me, "Anna, our path is different, and you suffer a lot. Why join now?" and within a few seconds, HE again said, "It is God's Design, and I send your brother, God Ganesh with you to remove obstacles which you encounter in coming days. He took a piece of mud, transforming it into Ganesh Idol. He kept me in my hand and virtually held it, and no sooner did it disappear from my hands. He blessed me and applied a red turmeric powder on my forehead. I soon realized that my entry into medicine would never be a smooth and peaceful journey but a horrifying journey with challenges, paradoxical events and many painful incidents.

Final Reflection: Embracing Divine Guidance

As I reflect upon the twists and turns of my journey, I am reminded of the profound truth that forces beyond our comprehension often shape our paths. Each challenge, setback, and miraculous encounter has been a testament to the intricate design of the universe and the divine guidance that permeates our lives.

Through the trials and tribulations, I have learned to surrender to the higher purpose that orchestrates our existence. Whether it be the pursuit of academic dreams or the quest for spiritual enlightenment, every step taken is imbued with meaning and significance.

In the face of scepticism and adversity, I have found solace in the unwavering faith that guides my footsteps. It is a faith that transcends the boundaries of human understanding and connects me to a higher power that whispers wisdom in the silence of my soul.

May my journey serve as a reminder that amidst life's uncertainties, there exists a guiding light that illuminates our path with love, grace, and divine intervention. Let us embrace each moment with gratitude and trust, knowing we are held in the palm of a compassionate universe that guides us ever closer to our true essence.

As we navigate the intricate tapestry of life, may we find solace in the presence of the divine and the realization that our souls are forever intertwined with the sacred dance of creation?

Let us walk in faith, knowing that our journey is but a small part of the grand symphony of existence orchestrated by the divine hand. In the end, may we find peace in the knowledge that we are beloved children of the universe, guided by the wisdom of the soul.

Journey Through the Crucible: Reflections on Medical Education

A Prelude to Turmoil

I never expected that my life would be such a horrifying memory before joining medicine. Contrary to my life at SV University, Tirupathi, I experienced a virtual hell both in the College and the Hostel. I was the only one who joined Medicine while about completing my M.Sc. in Psychology.

Encountering the Abyss: Trials in the College and Hostel

The lecturers glaringly looked at me, and some rebuked me and asked me to discontinue my course. I could see real cruelty in some of them; even traces of humanity were hardly visible to my inner vision. The roommates were quite indifferent and only had one senior who used to be close with me. Some were taking liquor in the rooms, and their dressing pattern was horrible. But I had no voice to resist them, and they were younger than me by many years. Some of them purposefully used to paste vulgar photos of women in the room as part of teasing me.

Navigating Dietary Restrictions and Financial Struggles

Food was a big problem in the Hostel, for all items contained both Garlic and Onion, and I never used them in my lifetime. One of the cooks used to serve food affectionately, and I confined myself to eating rice with curds or buttermilk.

Some people, gazing at my curled hair, treated me like Baba, but others felt my presence inconvenient. I realized that plain talk, openness, generosity in sharing what we have with others, and feeling great about others are things this world doesn't like or appreciate. I was an odd man out in their circle.

The second problem is the meagre money I used to carry, which needed to be increased to meet even basic needs. I occasionally visited nearby vegetarian hotels and enjoyed taking plain IDLIs and Chutney.

I got habituated to taking tea or strong coffee. To meet my hunger and to manage homesickness, I went to a family at Kurnool, which we had known for many years. I never knew they disliked me going to their home and staying. I faced insults but managed them since eating homely food was my priority. I felt homeliness in their presence and believed in their external smiles without cognizing hidden dislikes for my repeated presence in their home. They murmured that I had encroached on their privacy, but they all looked like my family. There are perception differences, and everything looked new to me, including the people and their changed attitudes and behaviour. The time moved quickly, but I got stuck without any momentum in LIFE. I need to be a better fit in this system, which Ego and Hypocrisy govern.

Trials and Tribulations: Struggles Within the System

My father, who kept his retirement benefits with my uncle, requested that he rotate for personal use and send minimal interest to me. But that never happened smoothly, and he used to send me after repeated reminders. I was not sharing my problems with my parents, for they suffer psychologically, and I thought that my problems, like a hungry stomach, giddiness, and headache due to a lack of food, were much better.

Wrong medication for my Epistaxis" (Nosebleed) by doctors, resulting in lots of health issues, is one of my worst experiences. One professor threatened that he would fail in his subject if I rejected his proposal to marry his sister. The answer to all the issues is my silent suffering without inviting for a quarrelsome situation. These were some of the most embarrassing events in my college life.

The only professor who had a special liking for me and the one who treated me like his son was Dr. Ramachandra Rao, Head of the Department of Medicine. He is exceptional, and such persons are a boon to medical fraternity. He happened to be my cousin's professor and had a special corner for me since I was closely associated with him. Occasionally, I visited his home, for I could feel divineness. He is the worshipper of Guru Raghavendra Swamy of Mantralayam, and I, too, had a fascinating lot for that God. Despite odd situations.

Illuminating the Path Ahead

Emerging from the crucible of medical education, I returned to Anantapur for my house surgery internship with a newfound sense of determination. As I journeyed back to familiar surroundings, the resonance of OM echoed in my ears, a reminder that even in the darkest of times, a thread of light is waiting to guide us forward.

Through the trials and tribulations, I gleaned invaluable lessons: resilience in the face of adversity, the power of silent suffering, and the transformative influence of divine connection. As I embark on the next chapter of my journey, I carry with me the understanding that amidst life's darkest moments, the promise of light exists, waiting to illuminate our path forward.

The challenges I faced during my medical education - from dietary restrictions and financial struggles to academic pressure and personal conflicts - were profound. Still, they also shaped me into the resilient individual I am today. Each trial and setback served as a stepping stone towards personal growth and enlightenment.

Journey of a Dedicated Doctor: Trials, Triumphs, and Integrity

Choosing the Path

After completing my MBBS, I had two options: one was to stay back in a rented room in Kurnool and prepare for PG, and the other was to prepare for PG by staying in my hometown, Anantapur. I preferred the latter since the food would be fine. My memory was fresh during the initial years after completing the course.

Navigating Challenges

The next year, I qualified but scored a rank that only fetched pre-clinical and para-clinical subjects. However, I was set on obtaining an MD in psychiatry, so I took several entrance examinations in vain. Hard work and the Grace of God alone are the keys to success.

Unexpected Opportunity

At one time, I qualified for psychiatry at NIMHANS in Bangalore. It was quite a surprise when they informed me to come for an interview within hours of the entrance exam. I didn't bring my certificates, so I rushed to Anantapur the same day for the interview the next day. With great expectations, I appeared for the interview. One of the interviewers asked a few sarcastic questions unrelated to the subject and questioned my reasons for pursuing medicine while studying psychology.

Facing adversity

Sometimes, the world looks unbelievable, and reasons for appreciation or intolerant expressions of vengeance make no sense. I was told he was a Brahmin hater, and I knew after the interview that I would not be on the selected list of PG Psychiatry. My classmate, a junior to me for many years while studying in high school, got selected for M.Ch., which disappointed me. Later, my mentor and the person whom I adore, like my elder brother and God incarnate Bhagwan Sriram Sir, told me I was equal to 1000 MDs and asked me to pursue General Medicine.

He mentioned my name and qualifications as an MD (General Medicine) on the covers containing letters written to me. I then strongly decided to do an MD in general medicine, and my mentor and professor, Dr. Rama Chandra Rao, also took the same course.

As a doctor, I could manage all cases if I did an MD (General Medicine). The goal was disastrous because I got all the pre-clinical, like Anatomy, Biochemistry, and physiology, and para-clinical, like pathology, pharmacology, and microbiology every year. My father once compelled me to join Pathology since my cousin studied the same course.

I sought the opinion of Dr. Rama Chandra Rao, who advised me to do so. I went for certificate verification, but before paying the fee, my inner conscience did not permit me since I promised Sri Ram Sir to do an MD in General Medicine. It was a humiliating atmosphere when I came back without joining the course.

My father scolded me, but I decided to continue my preparation, although my classmates completed one course and are pursuing additional courses. I told myself that the words given to Bhagwan should not be violated, irrespective of the outcome. Mine is a peculiar temperament, and sometimes I appear a specimen to the world of others. Changing myself and my mindset to appease others was not my nature, and I preferred to be what I wanted to be rather than what God wanted me to be.

During a visit to our home in Ram Nagar, we were honoured by the presence of SSS Vidyanarayana Theertha Yathi, a revered saint of the Modern Era from Badarika Ashram. During our interaction, someone graciously presented a book on Sai Baba, which he accepted with kindness. Upon inscribing it with the words "Beloved Nagaraj M.D. (Master of Divinity)," he offered comforting words that relieved the frustration caused by societal pressures related to professional degrees. His blessings proved to be a source of strength, sustaining me in the face of criticism from the world around me.

Divine Intervention

One day, I went to Pamidi for a function of a textile shop owner. It might have been his sister's wedding, but I don't remember the occasion.

Someone who looked like an Avadhooth told me by looking at me, in his words, "Good days are ahead of you. You will hear good news after you reach home". I was quite puzzled, and I came home with anxiety.

My father had just finished his pooja (prayer) and was hesitating to tell me I had received a registered cover from the Government of AP. He did not open it and was waiting for me to open it. When it opened, I was surprised that I got selected for the post of Assistant Civil Surgeon in the Anantapur district. It was through the APPSC selection process that I got a Government Job. My father was so happy to hear the news; he was joyful as it was a government job providing security.

Embracing Service

Years of waiting to get the PG seat without success and the uncertainty of getting it in the future made up my mind to join it. There were a few vacancies, but my father preferred Peddavaduguru PHC, near Gooty, where we have some landed property. I joined my Job and wanted to start a new life serving needy people.

I just learned that the Government Job involves many risks. The sisters and field staff were quite cooperative and liked me. I struggled with a few and didn't want to mention their names. My colleague, a lady doctor and a disbursing officer, was so jealous of me, and she continuously murmured, and her attitude was not good. I only say that it is essential for one to have a good character, but failing to do so will cause us to lose credibility in God's kingdom.

Later, I became a disbursing officer who was neither accustomed to taking bribes nor giving bribes. Even staff were gazing at me, for I never asked for a bribe for any work. I used to purchase medicine with my earnings since PHC sometimes doesn't supply medicines promptly.

I used to start my OP by 9.15 or 9.30, depending upon the availability of autos from PAMIDI, which I reached by bus, keeping my bicycle at the bus stand. My OP used to end by 3.30 or 4.30, depending upon the patients. People virtually worshipped me a lot and used to call me Baba Doctor since my bushy hair and a birthmark on my cheek resembled that of Baba.

I used to go out for fieldwork, and it was really a wonderful experience. I realized that there needs to be a higher level of health awareness and consciousness among people who consider having three square meals the first priority. I realized that people need care, compassion, and concern, which works wonders more than an injection or a pill. Becoming one with them is possible when we see the spirit of God present in them, and then, we feel their pain or pleasure.

There used to be a girls' residential school of government at Peddavaduguru, and I used to go there to treat girls and children suffering from ailments. The principal was also a devotee of Baba, and he used to treat me with all respect. Those days will not come again.

My mother used to prepare food for me and prepare a carrier for me daily, and I used to dine in a farmer's house known to me. I served them a little, and later, I took my food. Sometimes, people came to the house where I used to dine. I ran a clinic, and the patients bought medicine from the local medical store. I had a good name as a doctor and an honest person, and they told me that they never encountered a specimen doctor like me who knew how to serve without any expectations.

A Taste of Laughter: "What's Cooking?" with Amma

One day, I had a delightful conversation with my beloved mother, Karunamayi Amma (Venkata Lakshmi). My mother was always busy, tirelessly preparing dishes for her children without being asked. There was always a supply of food items, including pickles, powders, and other delicious treats.

As she went about her chores that day, I casually tossed out a Hindi phrase, "KHYA BATH HAI AMMA?" Translation: "What's up, Mom?" I repeated it a few times to make sure she heard, but she just looked puzzled and stayed silent. After a bit of persistence, she finally blurted out, "Why do you keep asking? It's VANGIBATH." Ah, VANGIBATH, she was cooking that delightful dish with rice, brinjal, potato, and capsicum. She thought I was asking about the food she was preparing and quickly responded, "VANGI BATH." Cue laughter! She couldn't understand why we found it so amusing until we explained the mix-up. Her confusion melted into a gentle smile. Whenever I need a mood boost, I revisit that memory. It's a moment that always brings joy and lifts my spirits.

Attitude of Higher Officials

The higher officials were not cooperative and used to insult me in meetings when I was not achieving family planning targets. The ulterior motto differs because I needed to provide a monthly fixed amount from my earnings, mostly unauthorized.

I was straightforward. When I spent part of my salary buying medicine, where would I get money to make such adjustments? I knew this after I left the position. One of the higher officials told one of the clerks, LALI Reddy, who was so honest and sincere.

When he went there for a signature, the higher official told him, "VADINI PATTUKONTE BHOODIDA RAALUTHUNDI," If I touch him, I need to collect VIBHOODHI, nothing else. Vibhoothi is a sacred ash I used to wear on my forehead every morning and even when I wash my face.

Divine Intervention: Embracing Opportunity on Sivarathri

The non-cooperation made me apply for a tutor post at the newly started Government Medical College. There were many vacancies, as government doctors did not prefer teaching since they were well-settled in private practice.

My maternal uncle and a doctor running a nursing home helped me get the post of anatomy tutor at Government Medical College, Anantapur. It happened on the day of Sivarathri, the festival I liked most.

I used to feel that I was the child of Lord Shiva and Goddess Bramaramba. I left my cosmic mother's lap long back to do something wearing this Body, and I realised that it hardly served even my kith and kin, with whom I had a previous association.

Challenges Faced

Sisters and a few staff associated with me at PHC, Peddavaduguru, shed their tears, for they loved me a lot, and it was a painful send-off. Before I finish, I recollect an incident where my colleague's doctor complained that I was taking bribes and unlearning authorized, including selling PHC medicine.

There were two groups in the village; one group supported her. The Government appointed a committee to probe into irregularities. Later, there was a big clash, and the enquiry committee members were not allowed to step down. They left listening to hundreds of people who gathered at PHC.

Resilience in Adversity

A journalist, closely allied with the lady doctor, fabricated false news about me to appease her. It served as a stark reminder of the treacherous nature of the world, where individuals manipulate truths to bolster their egos and agendas.

However, amidst the storm of deception, I witnessed the power of public sympathy and support rallying against those who sought to tarnish my character. It reinforced my belief in the potency of selfless work, detached from external authority, as a beacon of truth and integrity in a world often veiled in falsehoods.

It was a major factor in my shift to GMC, Anantapur. I never touched even the salary I earned, and I used to give it to my mother first, and later, my brother used to manage my little salary.

I used to take the amount from his packet after informing him and used to pay back the amount left after purchases. This is not to boost my image but to recall days of innocence or ignorance.

Sometimes, I thought I was not fit to be in this KALIYUGA where righteousness has no place and is covered by undeserving people. Good people like me had to suffer hell, for such people cannot compromise with the hard realities. Presuming that all that happened for my good only, I left the PHC Job at Peddavaduguru with a mixed feeling of joy and nostalgia to join as the Tutor in the Department of Anatomy, Government Medical College, Anantapur.

Spiritual Insights

In the sacred journey of life, I've realised a profound spiritual truth: amidst the trials and tribulations, souls hold a deep reverence for those adorned with genuine hearts overflowing with love, care, and compassion.

These ethereal beings cherish the selfless service of others as a divine gift, standing as radiant beacons of hope amidst the shadows of doubt. Their presence is a testament to our world's enduring power of goodness and kindness, illuminating our path with the divine light of compassion.

Through their divine example, we learn that even the smallest acts of kindness possess the transformative essence of the divine, capable of uplifting weary souls, healing wounded hearts, and igniting the flame of positive change. Their sacred presence is a gentle reminder of the interconnectedness of all souls and the boundless potential for spiritual growth and enlightenment within each of us.

Witnessing Life's Paradoxes: A Journey of Teaching and Spiritual Reflection

Embarking on a New Path

Farewell to PHC, Welcome to GMC: With heartfelt goodbyes, I departed from the Primary Health Centre (PHC) staff of Peddavaduguru, ready to embrace a new chapter as a tutor at Government Medical College (GMC), Anantapur. Despite numerous vacancies across various departments, I was assigned to the Department of Anatomy.

My spiritual mentor and brother, Dr. Sriram Sir, once mentioned that 'all your disappointments are God's appointments.' This phrase reflects a perspective that finds purpose and meaning in the challenges and disappointments we encounter in life. It suggests that what might initially seem like setbacks or letdowns could actually be part of a larger divine plan. It encourages trust in a higher power or a greater purpose behind the events that unfold in our lives, even if we don't immediately understand them. Essentially, it's about finding comfort and guidance in faith during difficult times, believing that there is a reason for everything that happens.

Guiding Through Life's Complexity

The Anatomy Lab and the Nauseating Reminder: The pungent aroma of formalin in the Anatomy Lab stirred memories of my medical student days, yet amidst this discomfort, I found solace in guiding students through the intricacies of human anatomy. Drawing from my struggles as a student, I endeavoured to make the subject more accessible and engaging for my students.

Sacred Connections and Innocent Seekers: Blessings and Encouragement: Some of my students, moved by sentiment, sought my blessings and requested the application of sacred vibhuti. Others, with innocence in their eyes, looked to me for reassurance and confidence before their examinations, eager for a few words of encouragement.

Navigating Intolerance and Unjust Accusations

The Sting of Unfounded Suspicion: Regrettably, certain staff members exhibited intolerance when female students sought my guidance, viewing me solely as a tutor and not acknowledging my dedication and expertise. This intolerance escalated when the department fell victim to theft, and unjust suspicion fell upon me, the bearer of a single set of keys.

Finding Joy in Giving

Generosity Amidst Dietary Restrictions: Despite my dietary restrictions, I enjoyed fostering a jovial atmosphere during practice sessions and generously providing refreshments for my students. The joy lay in their happiness rather than indulging in the offerings myself.

I spent money purchasing dusters, chalk-piece boxes, white markers, battery cells, and various other small items for the college. I didn't anticipate any praise from my superiors for the prizes I procured for students or my small college contributions.

Unfortunately, the higher-ups would deliberately criticize me, leaving me to ponder why they were so intolerant of these seemingly insignificant gestures that brought me immense satisfaction. Paradoxically, they all claimed to be spiritual and divine, yet their attitudes and actions betrayed a sense of malevolence. Intolerance, I've come to realize, is far more distressing than any physical ailment.

A Journey Through Transitions

From Microbiology to Anatomy and Back

I transferred to microbiology, where I learned new skills and excelled in teaching. I managed the lab with one or two technicians, finding fulfilment in nurturing the next generation of scientists. However, to my surprise, some orchestrated my transfer back to the Primary Health Centre under the jurisdiction of medical education.

The Unexpected Turn

Posted to BK Samudram, I felt a dark presence looming over my abrupt shift from the Medical College. It seemed as though someone had manipulated circumstances through witchcraft. Determined to seek clarity, I applied for long leave and travelled to Hyderabad to seek solace among my circle.

A Divine Intervention

During my time away, divine intervention appeared at play. Influenced by my connections and perhaps a higher power, the Director of Medical Education reconsidered and reassigned me to GMC, Anantapur, once again as a Tutor in Anatomy. It was more than a shock to those who thought I would nod and leave the college. They hardly realized that a Mighty Force accompanies me wherever I move.

Upon the principal's recommendation, I was surprised to notice that the district administration had chosen me for the Best Teachers Award. I felt that they had honoured God in me lately.

Navigating Ethical Dilemmas: A Personal Reflection

In the realm of office dynamics, certain individuals have wielded their authority to exploit and manipulate others. Such experiences can leave a lasting impact, especially when faced with the moral dilemma of succumbing to their demands or upholding one's principles.

In my own journey, I've encountered situations where office staff have attempted to coerce me into unethical dealings, leveraging the threat of professional repercussions. Despite my innate sensitivity to such matters, I found it challenging to grasp the extent of their insensitivity fully.

Thankfully, I had the counsel of my brother, Dr. Hari, whose wisdom provided a guiding light amidst the darkness. His suggestion to conceal any demanded amounts within a spiritual book offered a practical solution and a symbolic act of preserving integrity in the face of moral compromise.

However, the recurrence of such incidents left me feeling deeply troubled. No matter how discreetly executed, each instance of bribery underscored a troubling reality: the pervasive normalization of corruption within our societal fabric. It's disheartening to witness how individuals from all walks of life, regardless of their position, readily engage in such practices without hesitation.

Yet, amidst these challenges, I can't help but empathize with those who perpetrate such acts. Often, they are blinded by their own self-interest and fail to comprehend the profound repercussions of their actions. It's a cycle of ignorance that perpetuates harm, both to individuals and to society's collective moral conscience.

Throughout these trials, my primary focus remained on my mother's well-being. Her illness served as a stark reminder of life's fragility, overshadowing any personal grievances or struggles. Despite our hopes for her recovery, each glimmer of progress was met with a new wave of adversity, compounding her suffering.

In retrospect, these trials have deepened my understanding of ethical complexities and the importance of resilience in upholding one's values. While the allure of expediency may tempt us, our unwavering commitment to integrity ultimately defines our character and shapes our legacy. Moreover, I made the difficult decision to decline the promotion to Deputy Civil Surgeon due to my mother's illness, prioritizing my presence and support for her during her time of need.

A Quest for Justice: Battling Injustice in a Selfish World

Hope Crushed: Government Order (GO) Exclusion

Recognizing life's impermanence, I contemplated extending my work to support my brother, whose income is meagre. I noticed radiating rays from Sri Chandra Sekhara Paramacharya on 30th May 2018 from the photo at midnight three and the letters 63.

I followed news that mentioned the superannuation age increase for all doctors in the AP State. Hope arose when the government proposed extending the retirement age for doctors with MBBS qualifications to 63 years. I felt happy because my work in college would satisfy my soul while it would fetch income that would be helpful to my brother, who finds it hard to run the family with his earnings. Bhagwan Sathya Sai Baba also appeared in a dream and said, 'Work Done', which made me feel that the outcome would be positive. However, the subsequent Government Order (GO) unjustly excluded MBBS doctors from this provision.

Seeking Justice: A Lonely Battle

I planned to boost my low spirits by getting an opportunity to serve for three years, but nothing worked out. Seeking fairness, I turned to the Medical Association, but my pleas fell on deaf ears. Even the Association's President, a specialist doctor I knew, callously dismissed my concerns, suggesting I pay my way through. It was a stark reminder of the world's selfish nature, where self-interest reigns supreme. Upon my brother's counsel, I took legal action against the discriminatory GO, filing a case in the AP tribunal. Through this process, I understood the complexities of justice, where interpretations of law can vary widely. However, the wheels of justice turned slowly, leaving me disillusioned and drained.

COVID-19 Complications: The Weight of Injustice

COVID-19 added to the problems. The courts hardly functioned regularly, and everything was online. However, only a few could purchase justice online or offline. Only those blessed with perennial sources of unauthorized earnings could go to court, and those who toil hard for income to sustain themselves will only go bankrupt if they go to court. It is commonly said that justice delayed will be justice denied, and it's true. The court cases of innocents who richly deserve justice will hardly see the light.

A Fight for Dignity: Upholding Sacred Determination

Fuelled by false hopes from lawyers, the bitter taste of waiting only deepened my resolve to protect my dignity. Despite the world's perception of asking for help as a form of begging, my fight stemmed from a place of sacred determination.

Injustice Prevails: A Costly Struggle

In the harsh light of reality, my spirit wrestled with biased, discriminatory, and inhumane systems. Yet, ultimately, my struggle proved futile, a waste of time, money, and precious energy. It sapped out my stored-up energies to stretch my life with dignity.

Faith Amidst Injustice: Finding Meaning

Contemplating the purpose behind such events, I wondered why God designs incidents that degrade the purity of the soul. Though the answer eludes me, my faith remains unwavering, a guiding light amidst the darkness of injustice.

The Triumph of Integrity: A Spiritual Message

I knew with certainty that those who deceived me and callously insulted my soul would inevitably face the consequences dictated by the natural order. True to the workings of Natural Law, no one can evade justice, regardless of their apparent security in perpetrating injustice. This serves as a profound spiritual message, reminding us that integrity and kindness ultimately triumph over deceit and cruelty, even if the path to justice sometimes seems obscure.

A Legacy of Unfulfilled Aspirations

Dreaming of a Legacy

Despite my significant contributions to the college community, including providing various essentials, I harboured a simple yet heartfelt aspiration: refurbishing the room I once occupied. It was a dream infused with nostalgia and a desire to leave a lasting mark on the place that had been a significant part of my journey.

The Harsh Reality

However, as I sought to realize this dream, I encountered a disheartening reality. The association, administration, and other entities from which I had expected support and encouragement seemed indifferent to my aspirations. Their lack of assistance only deepened my disappointment and disillusionment.

A Reflection on Resilience

In the face of these setbacks, I found myself reflecting on my broader experiences. Success in worldly pursuits had never been elusive to me; instead, I had encountered numerous defeats and endured hurtful insults. Yet, amidst these challenges, one steadfast belief remained: my unwavering commitment to 'Truth'.

The Unwavering Commitment to Truth

Truth is not merely a concept to be acknowledged but a guiding principle that shapes my thoughts, words, and actions. Regardless of the falsehoods and manipulations that may pervade the world around me, I refuse to waver from this path of truth. It is a stance that requires courage and resilience, yet it is one that I embrace wholeheartedly.

Finding Solace in Integrity

In the face of disappointment and adversity, my dedication to truth remains unwavering. Though my dreams may be deferred and my efforts may go unrecognized, I take solace in knowing that I stand firmly on the side of honesty and integrity.

Trusting in Divine Plans

Despite the challenges and disappointments, divine plans transcend human limitations. As a silent witness to life's unfolding mysteries, I remain steadfast in my dedication to teaching and guiding the next generation of medical professionals. I always used to lower myself like a lay person, for there is pleasure in being unidentified by others by our inherent talents and skills.

Seeking Solace in a Spiritual Perspective

Despite offering my services wholeheartedly, without expecting anything in return, I received no response. It's disheartening to realize that sometimes, even when you extend kindness and generosity, people may still doubt your intentions. However, in the face of such skepticism, it's crucial to approach the world with a renewed spiritual lens, seeking deeper understanding and embracing compassion.

By looking at the world through a "renewed spiritual lens," one aims to find deeper meaning and insight. This might involve exploring questions of purpose, connection, and the nature of reality from a spiritual or philosophical standpoint. Additionally, the emphasis on "embracing compassion" implies the importance of empathy and understanding toward others, even when viewpoints may differ. It advocates for a holistic and empathetic approach to navigating life's complexities.

The Power of Divinity and the Enigma of Evil: A Journey of Spiritual Insights

Instances of individuals, predominantly women, embodying Sakthi, the supreme cosmic energy, are observed across various regions of the country, notably in Andhra Pradesh, Telangana, and Tamil Nadu. While some may prove to be counterfeit, the existence of genuine manifestations cannot be categorically dismissed. Human energy operates through seven fundamental chakras, familiar to most spiritual aspirants or sadhakas, ranging from Muladhara at the base to Sahasrara at the crown. Accounts of such phenomena abound in spiritual literature, with even renowned figures like Swami Vivekananda bearing witness to them.

The encounters with individuals possessed by Sakthi serve as reminders of the subtle ways in which the divine communicates with humanity. Trusting in the guidance of the divine, even when it seems mysterious or unconventional, can lead to profound spiritual growth and understanding.

During my upbringing in Mylavaram village, where my father served in the irrigation department,

I encountered such rare phenomena at a tender age. A certain individual, namely SUBBALAKSHAMMA, possessed by the cosmic mother, Sakthi, resided in a humble hermitage in a remote village near Mylavaram.

She would speak about me and my background, delving into subtle nuances of my life, seemingly unaware of her words while under divine influence. Her sole aspiration was devotion to the Cosmic Mother, devoid of material desires. These encounters instilled a profound trust in divine guidance, showcasing how the divine communicates with humanity in subtle and mysterious ways.

The selfless devotion of those possessed by divine energy highlights the importance of transcending material desires on the spiritual path. By cultivating a mindset of pure devotion and unconditional love, one can align more closely with the divine and experience its transformative power.

Similar incidents occurred in Guntakal, where a temple dedicated to Sakthi stood along the path to the Railway Quarters. One day, as I casually entered the temple, a lady with flowing hair addressed me as Raja.

Our ensuing conversation unveiled past events and foretold future encounters, deepening my connection with the divine. In that sacred space, I felt the invisible protection of Mother Sakthi enveloping me, reaffirming my belief that evil dissipates in the presence of divine union with the Cosmic Mother. It was a profound realization that in aligning ourselves with the higher energies of the universe, we can transcend the darkness of evil and find solace in the embrace of divine love.

Amidst these encounters, I grappled with the impact of evil, particularly during my formative years. However, interactions with spiritual mentors, including Bhagwan Sri Ram, revealed a profound insight—that evil, often misunderstood, holds a purpose within the divine plan.

Despite enduring treacherous events, I've come to accept God's inscrutable will, trusting in its capacity to refine and propel me forward on the path of spiritual evolution. This acceptance of divine will has allowed me to surrender to a higher purpose and trust in the ultimate benevolence of the universe.

A Journey with a Noble Soul

Chennamma Avva: A Beacon of Wisdom

Chennamma Avva, a revered figure from Kuntimaddi village near Ramagiri Mandal in Anantapur District, was a paragon of wisdom despite her lack of formal education. She established a humble temple for Goddess Muthyalamma beneath a neem tree near the RDT office, where her predictions and guidance were remarkably accurate.

The Divine Presence of NASANAKOTA MUTHYALAMMA

Chennamma Avva was a custodian of the NASANAKOTA MUTHYALAMMA deity, venerated by thousands across Andhra Pradesh and neighbouring Karnataka. Our family witnessed numerous miracles through her blessings,

which might seem like fanciful tales to those unfamiliar with them.

My brother, who faced repeated failures despite numerous interviews, sought her blessings before each one. In 1990, as he prepared for a final interview for a lecturer post at SK University, he asked for a blessing to secure the position. The possessed woman told him the post had already been promised to someone else and advised him to attend the interview without expectations.

She reassured him, saying, "Bala, I will see that you will be nearer to my temple soon." Although initially frustrated, my brother's patience was rewarded when he was appointed as Director in 1993 at the Rural Development Trust (RDT), an esteemed NGO working with the rural poor in Anantapur District. The RDT office was conveniently close to the temple, and all of her predictions came true, highlighting her profound spiritual insight.

Chennamma Avva: An Icon of Love and Service

Chennamma Avva's life embodied pure, selfless love. Despite her passing, which was marred by neglect and illness, her devotion and love left a lasting impact on our family. Her life mirrored that of Sabari Maa, reflecting a deep connection between suffering and divine purpose.

Her unfulfilled manuscript and the tragic loss of her grandson to COVID-19 only underscore the depth of her influence. Her presence continues to inspire, symbolizing the power of love and devotion in overcoming earthly struggles.

The Influence of Service and Devotion

My brother's fortunate placement in RDT, an organization founded by Father Vincent Ferrer and Sister Anne Ferrer in 1969, was seen as a divine blessing. The Ferrers, sent to transform Anantapur District—a region plagued by chronic drought—provided profound support and guidance. My family advised my brother to remain with the organization, emphasizing that the true dissolution of karma comes through service. This service is a manifestation of ultimate love.

Divine Providence and RDT:
A Journey of Faith and Transformation

The entry of my brother into RDT was a profound manifestation of Divine Providence, as acknowledged by Father Vincent Ferrer. Sister Anne nurtured him not only to become a skilled professional but also to work with a compassionate heart. Had he not been selected by RDT, his life could have taken a trajectory beyond our imagination. It is a testament to the divine will that orchestrates our destinies, weaving each thread with purpose and intention. RDT's continued commitment to its mission reflects the essence of this divine guidance, embodying the principle that goodness is a reflection of the divine itself.

Evolved Soul

Bhagwan Sriram affirmed Chennamma Avva's evolved soul and her significant role in our family's journey. Her enduring legacy serves as a beacon of divine grace and guidance, demonstrating that noble souls transcend the trials of life and continue to illuminate our paths with their wisdom.

Enduring Legacy of Divine Guidance

Through Chennamma Avva's life, I have learned that divine presence remains unwavering, even amid the most significant challenges. Noble souls, connected through past associations, provide us with light and understanding, acting as beacons of grace in a world often shrouded in darkness. Her story teaches that love and devotion, even when faced with adversity, can guide us towards spiritual enlightenment and resilience.

Mastering Concentration

Mastering Concentration: Your Path to Academic Excellence

In my interactions with medical students at Government Medical College, Anantapur, we delved into the profound impact of concentration on academic success. Allow me to share insights that can empower you on your educational journey.

Understanding Concentration

Many students face challenges with concentration, a crucial skill for success in any endeavour. Concentration, akin to the focused dedication of artisans like barbers, goldsmiths, and carpenters, is developed through disciplined practice. The mind, driven by the senses, constantly seeks stimulation. To control it, we apply 'Budhi', avoiding distractions ('DAMA') and maintaining inner calm ('SHAMA'). When mastered, a concentrated mind becomes a powerful tool for achieving great things. As Swami Vivekananda eloquently put it, a concentrated mind is like a searchlight, illuminating the path to success.

Insights from Ancient Wisdom

Ancient scriptures and teachings emphasize concentration as the key to unlocking mental potential. Patanjali's Yoga Sutras guide us to achieve mental equilibrium through disciplined practice.

Tranquil surroundings and Yogasanas aid in calming the mind and enhancing concentration. As the Bhagavad Gita states, "Yoga is the journey of the self, through the self, to the self," aligning body, mind, and spirit for sustained concentration and personal growth.

Wisdom from Great Personalities

Mahatma Gandhi stressed that concentration is essential for self-mastery, likening a scattered mind to a scattered sunbeam lacking intensity and integrity. Dr. APJ Abdul Kalam highlighted the role of focus and hard work in achieving goals, inspiring students to prioritize concentration in their academic pursuits.

Practical Strategies for Effective Study Habits

Creating a conducive study environment with a dedicated study table and focusing on a single topic for at least an hour enhances concentration. Establishing regular study schedules, avoiding distractions, and fostering a passion for learning are crucial. Engaging deeply with study materials through reading, reflection, and discussion promotes understanding and retention.

Nurturing Faith and Love for Learning

Having faith in oneself and cultivating a genuine love for learning serve as catalysts for concentration and academic success. Approach studies with enthusiasm and purpose to overcome challenges and achieve goals. This proactive attitude not only improves academic performance but also fosters personal growth and lifelong learning.

Inspirational Quotes

Swami Vivekananda's words resonate deeply: "Take up one idea. Make that one idea your life—think of it, dream of it, live on that idea." Committing wholeheartedly to goals fosters concentration and clarity of purpose.

Spiritual Insights

- **Ancient Wisdom:** Patanjali's Yoga Sutras teach that disciplined practice leads to mental equilibrium and heightened concentration.

- **Tranquility through Yoga:** Yogasanas and tranquil surroundings help calm the mind, fostering sustained focus and personal growth.

- **Inner Mastery:** Mahatma Gandhi emphasized that concentration is key to self-mastery, essential for achieving integrity and depth in life.

- **Purposeful Living:** Dr. APJ Abdul Kalam's words highlight how focus and diligence help us realize our dreams and goals.

Conclusion

Concentration isn't just about focusing—it's a transformative journey toward self-mastery and academic excellence. By blending ancient wisdom with practical strategies and insights from great minds, you can cultivate concentration as a fundamental pillar of your academic and personal journey. Let discipline, faith, and a love for learning guide you toward unlocking your full potential, both in academics and in life.

Listen to Your Heart: A Path to Love and Connection

In life, we often feel a tug-of-war between our hearts and minds. It's like they're singing different songs. The mind tends to focus on "I", nurturing our ego and making us feel like the hero. But the heart sings a different tune, one of "we", showering love and reminding us that we're all connected in something bigger than ourselves.

The mind is like a pool full of information and questions. It likes to analyze and understand things. But the heart? Well, it's more like an ocean, vast and deep, filled with love and capable of transformation.

Sometimes, our minds can cloud our hearts with doubts and illusions. We need to remember to listen to our hearts and instead get caught up in the complexities of the mind. But here's the thing: our hearts are the true source of love and compassion. They don't care about things like religion or social status. They know that deep down, we're all the same.

Our hearts break when we let our minds take over and play deceitful games. But when we stay true to our hearts, we feel connected to something greater, something divine. So, let's open our hearts and let in the energy of the universe. Let's remember that we're all in this together and that love is the most powerful force of all. Let's listen to our hearts and let them guide us on our journey.

Life is a History......Death is a Mystery!

Life is a history; death is a mystery. Death is an interval between two lives. Everyone fears it, trembles at the very word, dreads to see the dead body. God loves it. Man is frightened by the very thought of it. Man wants to run away from it desperately, but like a shadow follows an object beneath a light, death haunts him.

Time rings the death knell at the best of God's will. Everyone has to die, everyone must die, and everything has to perish. Sages and trees are free to live and die. From God, death takes an appointment for every creature and strikes at everyone uncaringly and unsparingly at the stipulated hour.

Death is a full stop to the sentence of life. Death opens the doors into the vistas of astral life in different dimensions. But it separates the person from the world in which he and his beloveds lived together, moved together, laughed together, and wept together.

The corpse, which is ready for the grave, is silent, unmoved, untouched, and non-reactive. Unlike sleep, death does not wake up the person into the world, but does so into different nether worlds! The corpse on the pyre is consigned to ranging fire that burns everything to ash.

Does Lord Shiva, the Pralaya deva, reside in the grave to indicate that it is the common meeting place of all those who are Sacred Grade? Does Rudra besmear 'Vibuthi or Bhasma' to beckon humankind to the transience of Karma Shariras?

All incarnations are Karana Shareeras with higher individual and cosmic consciousness and are beyond time, space, may, and matter. Earth lives and dies. Ether ever lives and never dies. Time is a healer of wounds. Death hits the closest of the close and dearest of the dear. Sorrow ever gnaws at the attached hearts. Gloominess as dark clouds grip the bereaved.

What this life is? What happens after the interval of death? No one knows. One cannot know. Those who can never know because God, the cosmic director and dictator, does not allow living beings to know.

A dead person sees his dead body, also sees his beloveds, speaks, wails, diffuses through, cries, and groans.

We can neither see nor hear the soul. Sphere is different, language is different. Those who are dead want their people to see them, hear them, and expect their people to recognize their torture and perspire and gasp to console their wailing beloveds and to wipe off streaming tears. Yet, the spirits are hopeless, snatched by Gods, and pulled farther and farther off their bodies and mourning kins.

Time dictates, and death executes. The world has created a history of life. God alone is the creator of death and its mystery. The more the human mind struggles to grasp the clues, the more the mystery of death eludes. The wheel of time revolves around human life.

Be aware of Death, and only then can you be aware of Life. Be unconsciously conscious of death; only then can you be consciously conscious of life. You cannot invent peace but discover it deep in thy spirit instead. If Life is sweet, death is sweetest. Life is an undying History, and death is an unyielding mystery.

Bhagwan Sri Ram "SIR": What I Heard, Knew, and Perceived Through the Soul

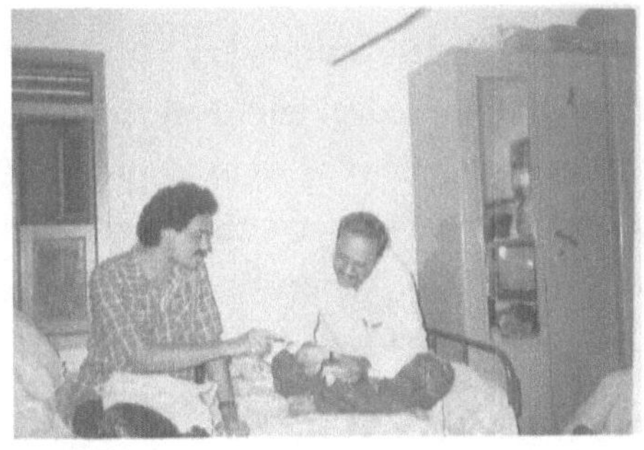

Bhagavan Sriram, affectionately known to His devoted followers as Sriram SIR, is revered as a living embodiment of divine grace. Believed by some to be a direct incarnation of Lord Srirama, by others as Lord Krishna, and by a few as the Lord of Seven Hills, His true divine nature remains a profound mystery. Just as Shirdi Sai appeared to some as Ganesh and to others as Dattatreya or Hanuman, Sriram SIR manifests differently to those who worship Him in various forms.

For over three decades, He has been residing in Hyderabad, living a simple life while fostering a deep sense of unity among His followers despite His significant respect within spiritual circles. Sriram SIR humbly asserts that He is not fundamentally different from anyone else.

However, the wisdom reflected in holy scriptures across various faiths, along with His unique presence, highlights His extraordinary nature. Those who have witnessed or heard of His miracles have only glimpsed a fraction of His boundless divine essence. He teaches that true spirituality is defined by unity and harmony.

His way of life exemplifies the art of living, and his teachings reflect the essence of the Bhagavad Gita. Sriram SIR defines spirituality as more than the mere affirmation of transient joys; it is the art of transforming fleeting joys into a lasting sense of fulfilment.

He emphasizes that true spirituality involves transcending conventional knowledge and embracing a profound state of unawareness about what is commonly understood. The statement means that true spirituality is not about acquiring more information or adhering to conventional wisdom.

Instead, it involves going beyond the surface level of common understanding and cultivating a deeper, often intuitive sense of awareness. This "profound state of unawareness" refers to shedding preconceived notions and everyday knowledge that might limit deeper spiritual insight. By doing so, one opens themselves to a more profound, often transformative, spiritual experience that transcends ordinary comprehension. Essentially, it's about letting go of what is commonly known to reach a deeper, more enlightened state of being.

He observes that modern individuals often feel unfulfilled despite many comforts because genuine joy is missing. This absence, he suggests, stems from a loss of wonder and curiosity. To reconnect with one's true self, one must cultivate innocence, which involves a deliberate ignorance of what is generally known to others.

Our sacred texts suggest that fully grasping the depth of the Vedas might take numerous lifetimes. Similarly, understanding the essence of Sriram Sir may take an entire lifetime, with unravelling His philosophy potentially requiring several more. Appreciating His divine influence over our lives might extend beyond this current existence. His divine nature is so profound and transcendent that truly comprehending it is a journey that spans lifetimes and beyond.

A Divine Introduction

In the 1950s, Lord Hanuman graced the dream of a devout Sadhu in Tanuku, Andhra Pradesh, and revealed that Bhagavan Sriram Sir would soon incarnate on Earth in Maldakal, Telangana. This prophecy came to fruition when Sriram Sir was born on May 11, 1957, in Maldakal. Originally named 'Sreeramulu,' He is now reverently known as Dr. Sriram, G. His followers, deeply touched by His divine grace, affectionately call Him "Bhagwan Sriram Sir," a testament to their profound reverence.

Dr. Sriram, G, a loving husband and father, is also a nature enthusiast, seeker of peace, and an esteemed global speaker. His academic journey is marked by a degree in sciences from M.A.L.D College, Gadwal, and an M.A. and PhD in English from Osmania University. Despite his academic brilliance and potential for a high-ranking civil service career, he chose a humble path as an English Lecturer, retiring in 2015 after a fulfilling 44-year career.

His seminal work, 'Viveka Sravanti' (later renamed 'Journey into Joy'), was praised by former President of India Dr. Shankar Dayal Sharma as being as profound as the Bhagavad Gita.

Bhagwan Sriram Sir conducts national and international workshops on different life-related subjects. He is a spiritual scientist, psychologist, philosopher, poet, author, and sage. His profound research into spirituality and joyful living, validated through his own transformative experiences, offers tools to enhance spiritual intelligence and find inner peace. He has authored several influential books, including 'Dew Drops on a Lotus Leaf,' 'Voyage into Consciousness,' and 'Journey into Joy,' each reflecting his deep wisdom and spiritual insight.

Personal Reflections

My introduction to Bhagwan Sriram SIR came through my younger brother Ganesh in 1986. Initially, my brother spoke of Him as the "Mysterious Spiritual Man" (MSM) and did not reveal His name. From the moment I encountered Sriram Sir, I felt an indescribable connection, as if our souls were intertwined from past lifetimes. My family and I hold a deep belief that my elder brother Srinivasulu—a born yogi who departed this world at a tender age—is reborn as Sriram Sir. This belief is deeply personal and beyond the scope of debate.

While with Bhagwan Sriram Sir in Nizamabad, I experienced the profound bliss of being in His divine presence. I cherish these moments as a precious gift. His visits to our home, which we lovingly call "OM," and our shared meals, like jowar roti with brinjal curry, were moments of divine joy. He often spoke of finding happiness in the simple joys of life, such as savouring a meal and marvelling at the beauty of the cosmos.

He wrote several letters to me and my siblings, some of which are personal and not intended for circulation, while others have been published in his work *Viveka Sravanthi*. I have always cherished the moments spent in his presence and the opportunities to interact with him. A particularly memorable experience was accompanying him to Puttaparthy, where I had the privilege of sitting beside him and witnessing the divine glory of Bhagwan Sri Sathya Sai Baba. In my joy, I would often hug him and, in a burst of exuberance, lift him up, fully aware that he is the uplifter of souls entangled in the illusions of KALI Maya.

Writing letters to Sriram Sir became a vital outlet for my emotions, whether in times of joy or distress. He received these letters with boundless patience, often feeling as though He was reading reflections of His own experiences. Our bond transcends this lifetime, giving me unwavering solace and strength through life's trials. Despite some advice to cease my correspondence, those who suggested this could not fully understand the depths of my soul's struggles. To me, Sriram Sir is not just a divine presence but a cherished friend and brother, offering support and understanding through every challenge.

He knows me intimately, and I know Him profoundly; together, we share a sacred and transformative connection that transcends ordinary understanding. This profound spiritual bond reflects a divine unity where our souls are harmoniously aligned. Our relationship embodies spiritual oneness, with each of us deeply attuned to the other's essence. Through this mutual recognition, we embark on a profound journey of enlightenment, bound by a sacred truth that surpasses the limitations of time and space. Our connection is a living testament to the divine harmony that links our spirits, guiding us toward a shared realization of higher truths.

Whispers of the Night: Finding Harmony in the Silence of Solitude

The Interplay of Soul, Mind, and Medicine

Choosing medicine was not merely a professional decision but a quest to understand the profound connection between Soul, Mind, Body, and Medicine. The journey towards inner peace begins with the detoxification of the mind. We face a crucial choice in life: embracing positive or negative thinking. Negativity draws harmful elements such as microbes, oxidants, and toxins, which impair our organs and weaken the immune system. Conversely, positive thinking enhances cellular protection, stimulates healing proteins, and produces antioxidants that boost immunity and accelerate recovery.

The Bhagavad Gita provides a timeless example of this principle. Lord Krishna advises Arjuna to transcend material dualities and align his actions with his higher self. Krishna's guidance emphasizes that a positive, detached mindset supports both physical and spiritual well-being. Just as Arjuna was guided to maintain inner peace amidst external chaos, we, too, must cultivate positivity to foster healing and balance in our lives.

The Power of Positive Thinking

Evaluating our thoughts and emotions is essential for making balanced decisions. The synergy of Soul, Mind, and Body can diminish the need for medication and promote rejuvenation through meditation. Nourishing the body extends beyond food; it encompasses what we hear, see, and speak internally and externally.

Rumi, the great Sufi poet, beautifully illustrates this concept. His poetry often reflects the harmony between the soul and the divine. Rumi teaches that aligning our inner thoughts with divine love transcends worldly suffering, leading to tranquillity and understanding. This alignment reinforces the importance of maintaining a positive mindset for inner peace and holistic health.

The Role of Spiritual Practices in Health

Health is profoundly connected to soul consciousness. Engaging in spiritual practices such as KRIYA Yoga, Heartfulness Meditation, OM Shanti Meditation, or Patanjali's Yoga techniques activates the ultimate source of energy for health and well-being. By immersing ourselves in these practices, we transform body consciousness into soul consciousness.

These practices echo the spiritual teachings found in epics. For instance, Patanjali's Yoga Sutras underscore the significance of mental discipline and meditation in achieving a balanced state of being. We tap into transformative energy by adopting these spiritual practices, aligning ourselves with holistic health.

Learning from Nature

Nature offers profound lessons in the art of living and inner engineering. Transforming body consciousness into soul consciousness involves recognizing that good intention surpasses the mind, good thought exceeds intention, and meditation transcends thought. Spiritual texts suggest, "Meditation reveals the soul," emphasizing that reverence for intention and meditation aligns with divine attributes.

In the Bhagavad Gita, Krishna encourages Arjuna to observe nature's patterns to understand the divine order. Nature's cycles and rhythms—such as the changing seasons—provide insight into maintaining balance and harmony. By attuning ourselves to nature's wisdom, we gain a deeper understanding of how to align with our higher selves.

The Supremacy of Divine Presence

Recognizing the infinite Supreme Force within us renders fear irrelevant. Embracing God, the essence of the Supreme Creator becomes our sole hope. Spiritualists often retreat into nature to uncover life's truths, finding that nature reveals itself to receptive ones. The more we align with nature's benevolence, the richer our experience becomes.

This notion is mirrored in Rumi's teachings, which emphasize the divine presence within and around us. Rumi's poetry encourages us to align with this divine essence to transcend fear and find solace in our connection with the Supreme.

The Duality of Ego and Humility

The "Big I" symbolizes ego, while the "small i" represents humility. The ego arises from body consciousness and lacks soul, whereas the small "i" embodies the spiritual life force. Ego is an illusion born of ignorance, akin to a candle's fleeting light. Festivals like Holi remind us to embrace humility and holiness.

The Bhagavad Gita addresses Arjuna's ego and underscores the importance of humility and self-awareness. We align more closely with our true nature and spiritual purpose by overcoming ego and embracing humility.

Insights from the "Mind the Mind" Workshop

Although I did not attend Bhagwan Sri Ram's "Mind the Mind" workshop, my soul grasped its essence through reflection. The workshops emphasize taking personal responsibility for one's life and focusing on self-improvement rather than attempting to change others. Dr. Sri Ram Sir's teachings suggest that while creation remains constant, true change occurs in our perceptions and personal growth. The natural world around us beautifully illustrates this idea.

Consider the example of a river. A river flows steadily, adapting to the landscape it encounters. It doesn't attempt to change the mountains or valleys but instead moulds itself around them, shaping its course as it moves forward. Similarly, we must focus on our growth and adapt our perceptions rather than trying to control or alter external circumstances. By doing so, we align ourselves with the natural flow of life, fostering personal transformation and harmony.

Another vivid example can be drawn from the growth of trees. Trees do not alter the soil or weather to suit their needs. Instead, they adapt to the environment, drawing nourishment and strength from it to grow and thrive. This mirrors the concept that true change comes from within. As trees adapt to their surroundings, we must nurture our personal growth and adapt our perspectives to align with our higher selves.

Bhagwan SRI RAM SIR's teachings resonate with the principle that while creation remains constant, our growth and change come from how we perceive and interact with the world. By enhancing our existence, much like how a river or tree aligns with its environment, we foster a deeper sense of fulfilment and inner peace.

A Silent Dialogue with the Soul

During my late-night walks on the balcony, I enter a serene realm of reflection as I breathe in the crisp, refreshing air. The stillness of the night offers a rare opportunity for deep introspection and joy. With the day's busyness behind me, I sense a profound connection with the trees and flowers surrounding me. Their silent whispers resonate with my heart, the flowers speaking to me through their vibrant colours and delicate petals. The cool breeze soothes my tired soul, while the touch of tender leaves feels like caressing a smiling child, igniting memories of innocence and joy.

The Rhythm of Nature

What miracles do we need more than the blossoming flower? A flower transforms into a bud, and then that bud develops into fruit, each with varying tastes. There is so much rhythm in nature, and understanding its essence is simple. Yet, we complicate it with our complex mindsets. In this cacophonic world, spending time with nature in the absence of crowds and noise feels like being embraced by Mother Nature herself—ever loving, never hurting, and always giving.

A Cosmic Connection

As I gaze at the stars and the moon, I am reminded of my true home, the abode from which I came before reaching this earthly realm. In these celestial moments, I feel as if the universe is conveying messages of love and guidance. The memories of times spent with my beloveds linger in my mind, evoking warmth and nostalgia. Yet, I cannot ignore the sufferings of my sister, father, brother, and mother, which once weighed heavily on my heart. My inability to address their pain often left me feeling uncomfortable and restless.

Joyful Laughter

Sometimes, my brother's subtle jokes flash through my mind, causing me to laugh loudly, even in the quiet of the night. He used to tease me, hinting that the neighbours might wake up and gaze out at the source of my laughter. I would respond, "Leave me 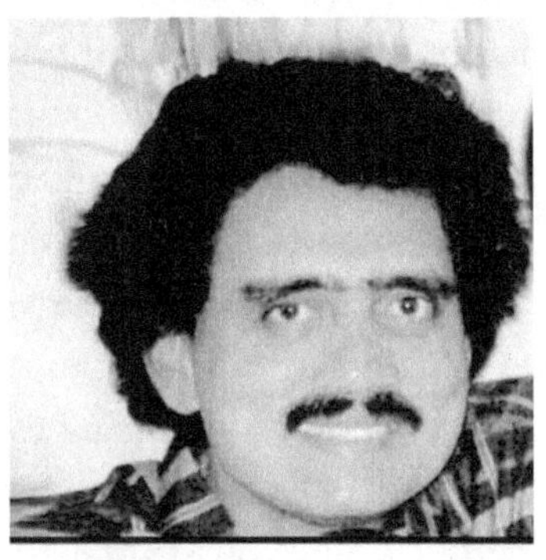 alone! There's a joy that keeps my spirits vibrant." Letting out emotions is key to maintaining mental equilibrium, and these moments of joy remind me of the bond we shared.

Cultivating Empathy and Spiritual Growth

In our journey through life, it is vital to forget the good we've done for others but never to forget the kindness we've received. Respond with empathy, for true joy is not found in material wealth or sensory pleasures but in inner transformation and alignment with the world's natural rhythm. Life itself is simple, but it is our perceptions that complicate it. Living with simplicity and common sense strengthens our inner resolve, allowing us to navigate life's challenges with greater clarity and wisdom. "Simplicity is the ultimate sophistication," Leonardo da Vinci once noted, urging us to embrace the beauty of a straightforward life.

Bhagwan Sri Ram's teachings remind us to seek the unity of soul, mind, and body. When we do, we live in harmony not only with ourselves but with the divine presence that resides in all things. Insights from spiritual epics and personal experiences alike tell us that true growth comes from cultivating empathy and embracing a life of simplicity and service. Each act of kindness and every moment of reflection brings us closer to the essence of our being, guiding us toward a life that is spiritually enriched and divinely aligned. Thich Nhat Hanh wisely said, "When you plant lettuce, if it does not grow well, you don't blame the lettuce. You look for reasons it hasn't grown well. It may need fertilizer, or more water, or less sun. You never blame the lettuce." Likewise, when the soul doesn't blossom as expected, it is not the soul to blame. Instead, we must reflect on the nourishment it receives— perhaps it longs for stillness, deeper communion with the divine, or a return to simplicity. Just as a plant needs the right balance of sunlight and water, the soul requires love, peace, and spiritual attention to thrive. Blaming the soul only distances us from its true nature; understanding and nurturing it brings us closer to divine alignment."

The Journey of the Soul

In fact, I like darkness because I can see the light in it. There is no competition; each plant gives birth to different flowers, each unique in size, colour, and fragrance. In today's unhealthy competitive landscape, I sometimes feel like a redundant person. I wonder at the gradual changes in the values of the students I once taught. In the beginning, there were those who paid close attention, preparing diligently for each lesson. Over time, however, I noticed a shift.

Reflections on Education

Students began skipping classes, drawn away by entertainment or the pressure of preparing for postgraduate studies, even from their very first year. I find myself questioning the quality of learning we can expect when days have become so machine-dependent. The goal of every student seems to be getting a postgraduate degree and starting private practice. While I don't say this is inherently wrong, it makes me reflect on the essence of learning.

The Journey of Learning

Learning is a journey, not merely a destination. Yet, in this race, we now see an abundance of doctors, more patients, an increase in diseases, countless investigations, more money, more debts, and, unfortunately, more unhappiness. This paradox of our times—where convenience often trumps depth—leads us to wonder if we truly understand the purpose of our pursuits.

In earlier days, doctors of divine virtue could diagnose even critical illnesses simply by touching the pulse. There was a profound connection between healer and patient, rooted in understanding the whole person. Now, with the rise of specialization, we face a disintegration between each system, and somewhere along the way, the modern medical system seems to have lost its way. I feel deeply about these changes, yet I remain silent, for I cannot speak my truth; degrees matter more than wisdom.

Sometimes, I find myself contemplating a different path—I should have become a homeopathic doctor, like Samuel Hahnemann, the father of homeopathy. However, I've come to realize that even homoeopathic practitioners often succumb to the same pressures as their allopathic counterparts. The ultimate goal seems to shift towards profit, capitalizing on the suffering of patients. This reveals a deeper issue: we lack true integration in our society, which is divided by numerous forces. Likewise, our thinking often lacks integrity, existing in bits and pieces rather than as a cohesive whole.

This is not an appeal for sympathy but rather a call for greater empathy towards those who suffer beyond our comprehension. In a world filled with advancements, let us not forget the human aspect of healing. Let us strive to connect with the essence of our practice, nurturing not only the body but the spirit of our patients.

A Life of Thanksgiving

Ultimately, life is a Thanksgiving ceremony—a continuous celebration of existence. Let us take a moment to thank everyone and everything around us, from the humans who touch our lives to the nature that nourishes our souls. Each encounter, every breath of fresh air, and the simple beauty of a flower remind us of the interconnectedness of all things. In acknowledging the gifts life bestows upon us, we open our hearts to gratitude and compassion.

As we embrace this journey, may we express our heartfelt thanks, not only for the joy and beauty but also for the challenges that shape us. Let our lives be a reflection of gratitude, where every act becomes a tribute to the divine, and every moment is cherished as a blessing. In this way, we truly honour the essence of life, creating a ripple of positivity that resonates through the cosmos.

Life, indeed, is a ceremony of thanks—let us participate fully, embracing every moment as a sacred gift.

Embracing the Journey

As we navigate the complexities of life, let us remember that every experience, whether joyful or challenging, serves a purpose in our soul's journey. Embrace simplicity and cultivate empathy, for these virtues enrich our existence and connect us to the greater cosmos.

May we find clarity in moments of stillness and foster kindness in our interactions. Let our lives be a testament to gratitude, where each day is seen as a gift and each encounter as a blessing.

Ultimately, as we celebrate the beauty of our unique paths, may we understand that life is not merely a series of events but a profound journey of love, learning, and connection. Together, let us walk this path with open hearts, inspiring one another to illuminate the world with our light, creating a legacy of compassion and joy that resonates through eternity.

Transformative Spiritual Journey Under His Holiness Sri Sri Sri Kalluru Venkata Narayana Swamy: The Story of Guru Prasad

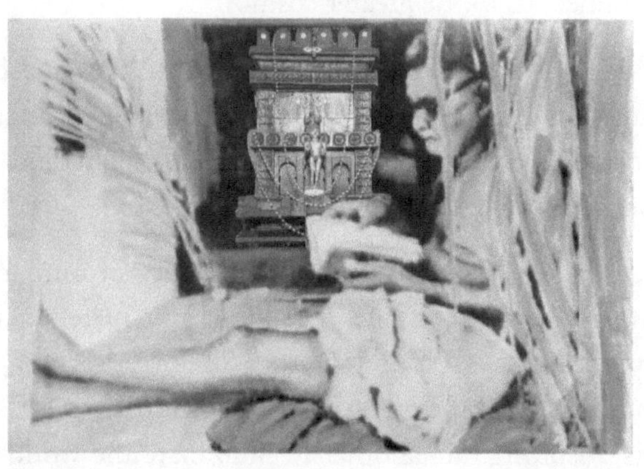

In the vast tapestry of spiritual traditions, few journeys stand as luminous and transformative as that of His Holiness Sri Sri Sri Kalluru Venkata Narayana Swamy and his disciple, Guru Prasad, who played a pivotal role in carrying forward the legacy. This narrative is not merely a recounting of miraculous events but a profound testament to a true Guru's boundless grace and wisdom. Swamy's life, marked by unparalleled scholarly achievements and divine encounters, serves as a beacon of inspiration. The legacy of Swamy, vividly illustrated by the dedicated and devoted Guru Prasad, continues to inspire and guide spiritual seekers, demonstrating the power of unwavering devotion, humility, and the transformative influence of spiritual guidance. As we delve into their journey, we are not only invited but also encouraged to embrace the timeless teachings that transcend the physical realm, leading us towards spiritual enlightenment and the realization of our inner divinity.

******

A Luminary in Both Scholarly and Spiritual Realms

His Holiness Sri Sri Sri Kalluru Venkata Narayana Swamy, born on March 6, 1902, in Bandamidpalle, Anantapur District, was a beacon of wisdom and spirituality. Hailing from the Badaganadu Niyogi sect, he displayed remarkable talent early on, mastering multiple languages and earning MAs in English, Telugu, and Kannada. His scholarly pursuits were academic and spiritual, as he had profound divine experiences, notably a divine vision of Guru Raghavendra

Swamy of Mantralaya, who bestowed sacred padukas upon him. This pivotal event, a testament to his shared divine connection, marked the beginning of Swamy's extraordinary spiritual journey. These profound spiritual experiences not only connect us to Swamy's journey but also intrigue us to learn more about his teachings and their transformative power.

A Life of Dedicated Service and Spiritual Depth

Swamy's career in education began in 1925, leading him to prominent roles such as Deputy Inspector of Schools and District Education Officer. His dedication to education spanned multiple districts until his voluntary retirement in 1956. Despite his forthright and occasionally quick-tempered nature, Swamy's life was deeply rooted in spirituality. He was a remarkable artist and writer, an advanced spiritual soul, and a god incarnate. As a testament to his spiritual depth, he established Guru Raghavendra Swamy Brundavana shrines in three locations, Railway Kondapuram, Isurallapalli, and Tadakaleru. These spiritual sanctuaries, not only guide and inspire his followers but also stand as physical manifestations of his profound spiritual journey, serving as beacons of his spiritual legacy.

The Hidden Depths of a Divine Incarnation

Swamy's true spiritual essence was discernible to only a few, with many devotees perceiving him as a divine incarnation. One such devotee was Guru Prasad, the spiritual successor of Tadakaleru Ashram. Initiated into spiritual practice at the tender age of seven, Prasad experienced numerous miracles that underscored the power and grace of his Guru. His life transformed dramatically through mantra sadhana and spiritual penance, showcasing the profound impact of Swamy's teachings.

Divine Transformations and Miraculous Encounters: The Spiritual Journey of Guru Prasad

Guru Prasad's journey is defined by extraordinary miracles reminiscent of Sai Baba, including the manifestation of vibhuti, idols, and salagramams.

His spiritual encounters with revered figures like Sai Baba of Shirdi, Ganapathi Sachidananda Swamy, and Kanchi Swamy Chandrasekhara Saraswati underscored the spiritual potency of Swamy's blessings. Prasad's experiences included transforming sand into sacred ash, enduring immersion in boiling oil unharmed, and averting calamities for his disciples. Among his most astounding miracles was the emergence of the sacred Triveni from his toe, symbolizing the convergence of spiritual energies.

Prasad displayed mystical prowess by traversing to the Himalayas, Shirdi, and Mantralayam in an instant, reminiscent of space travel, where he received the darshan of his Gurudev and parents. Encounters like seeing Shirdi Sai Baba physically in a garden at Shirdi and Baba's direction to go to the Himalayas culminated in his spiritual penance.

Guru Raghavendra Swamy blessed him invisibly by placing Kalakanda (crystal sugar) and Matrashitalu, directing him to Ganadhala, a holy shrine of Panchamukhi Hanuman. This temple holds immense spiritual significance near Bhikshalaya, where Saint Sri Raghavendra Swamy performed penance for twelve years.

The Divine Revelation: Guru Prasad's Spiritual Journey

Guru Prasad once confided in me that his Gurudev had instructed him not to showcase supernatural abilities until he received proper ordination publicly. During his spiritual gatherings, he often spoke with a sense of detachment, attributing his words to the divine guidance of his guru. Initially, he struggled to control the mystical phenomena manifesting in his hands and body. Fragrant vibhuti would spontaneously emanate, covering him entirely in a display beyond his control.

He humbly admitted the difficulty in managing the expectations of those around him, as many sought only miracles from him. Guru Prasad consistently emphasized that every experience and accomplishment was solely due to the grace of his Gurudev. Without his guru's initiation and guidance, he considered himself simply Guru Prasad, a vessel for his guru's divine will.

His journey was one of profound surrender and devotion, where every action and manifestation became a testament to the transformative power of divine guidance and surrender.

The Holy Shrine of Tadakaleru

As His Holiness Sri Potuluri Veera Brahmendra Swamy mentions, the Tadakaleru shrine holds significant spiritual importance. The Brundavan of Raghavendra at this holy shrine is exceptionally powerful, accompanied by the presence of Vibhudeswara Swamy and the Serpent God. Additionally, the Samadhi of Swamy's son, a born Avadhootha, is situated next to the Navagraha idols, further sanctifying the location. The shrine, located on the outskirts of Anantapur Town, remains a hidden gem known to few but holds extraordinary spiritual power.

During the temple's renovation, masons reported hearing Vedic hymns, a testament to the sacred energy permeating the site. The shrine's Kshetrapalaka (guardian deity) is Hanuman, who appears lively to devotees as they approach. The life-size photos of Swamy exude a sense of his omnipresence and omnipotence, reinforcing the need to protect the temple's sacredness and continue its spiritual legacy.

Humility and Spiritual Wisdom

Despite the miraculous phenomena surrounding him, Guru Prasad remained humble, attributing all his actions to the grace of his Guru. He emphasized that true spiritual power lies in humility and the constant remembrance of the Guru's presence. Prasad's visits to Kovela were marked by profound spiritual discussions, offering guidance and support during challenging times.

Literary and Spiritual Contributions

Swamy's literary contributions include works like Satyanaarayana Mahatmyamu, Aanjaneya Stavakalaamalika, Maanasabodha, and Krishnaraajuniyamu, authored in his childhood. His Telugu commentary for the Sri Raghavendra Stotra and his play Ahalyaasamkrandanamu, written at 19, highlight his literary prowess. His Telugu notes, published in 1928 as Andhra Vaajmayacharitra Sangrahamu, became a renowned critique and a textbook for the Vidwan exam for 30 years. Swamy wrote over twenty-five works, showcasing his natural flair for extemporaneous composition in poetry and prose.

Growth of Ashram: Role of Guru Prasad

Guru Prasad dedicated himself to developing Tadakaleru Ashram, where Swamy's samadhi and various sacred idols, including a rare idol of Shirdi Sai Baba and Mother Indrakshi, are enshrined. His efforts in nurturing the ashram reflect his unwavering devotion to his Guru and his mission to spread spiritual awareness.

The personal experiences of Swamy's devotees, including my mother's, vividly illustrate the enduring spiritual presence of Kalluru Venkata Narayana Swamy. During her admission to the ICU in Bangalore, my mother had a profound encounter: Swamy appeared near her bedside, moving around her before finally merging into the divine presence of Guru Prasad. These encounters poignantly underscore the miraculous and compassionate nature of Swamy's legacy, offering solace and guidance to those in need.

A Spiritual Message: Embrace Humility and Devotion

Swami's teachings emphasized the importance of humility, vigilance against ego, and the continuous engagement of disciples in spiritual practices. Guru Prasad's experiences serve as a reminder of the ever-present challenges posed by Maya (illusion) and the necessity of steadfast devotion to the Guru.

Embracing the Path of True Spirituality

The life and legacy of Kalluru Venkata Narayana Swamy embody the profound impact of a true spiritual master. His teachings, miracles, and literary contributions continue to inspire and guide countless seekers on their spiritual journeys. Swamy's divine presence felt through his disciple Guru Prasad and the sacred spaces he established, offers wisdom and solace to those who seek the truth.

Resuming the Spiritual Journey: Embracing Divine Guidance

I often counselled Prasad to be vigilant of pseudo-disciples around him, for they fail to grasp the profound power embodied in Guru Prasad, each one subtly aspiring to replace him, driven by the deceptive allure of Maya. The role of a Guru is exceptionally arduous, akin to handling a double-edged sword, fraught with challenges and responsibilities. I always envisioned Lord Shiva within Guru Prasad and frequently asked him if he could perceive this divine presence within my heart. I intended to share my innermost feelings with Prasad, hoping to support him on his spiritual journey. I wanted to help him remain grounded in the world while nurturing a deep sense of inner detachment. By doing so, I believed he could balance worldly engagement and spiritual transcendence.

"Guru Prasad, my profound message resonates with seekers of truth. I know you, and you know who I am. It would be best not to halt your spiritual journey; you must resume where you left off. Your SWAMY, Your PEDDANANNA, is the Doer. While we live in the world, we mustn't allow the world to overshadow us, just as a boat must stay afloat on the water without letting the water seep in. Though the Almighty may block my inner power for reasons best known to them, I earnestly wish for you to embark on higher spiritual endeavours, embrace the ASHRAM, and become His instrument in fulfilling HIS mission. May TADALAERU Holy Shrine radiate and illuminate the darkness of ignorance for millions. Swamy resides profoundly within every heart, but through deep communion with Him, we can navigate the tumultuous seas of life and reach HIS shore."

Divine Footsteps: The Mystical Journey of SRI SRINIVASA Swamy of Veparala

The Divine Origin of Swamy

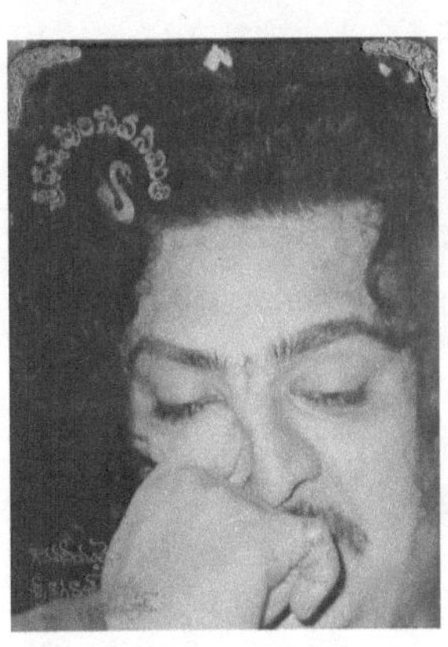

Swamy stands as a unique figure within his family lineage, bearing the unmistakable mark of divine purpose. It is said that incarnations choose the wombs of mothers according to their own divine will, manifesting on Earth for a specific mission, only to withdraw once that mission is fulfilled. Born in the sacred land of Veparala, nestled near the Mylavaram Dam, YSR Kadapa District, Swamy's earthly journey began with an air of mystique.

Close Encounters with the Divine

I had the privilege of walking the same paths as Swamy during our school days, attending the very institution where his youthful footsteps echoed. My visits to his abode in Veparala brought me closer to his family, forging bonds of kinship that would last a lifetime. Witnessing Swamy in his formative years and observing his growth over time, I became privy to the unfolding of his divine nature.

The Divine Education

Though Swamy's formal education may have taken a backseat, he embarked on a journey of unparalleled spiritual enlightenment. Gifted with the ability to communicate fluently in all languages, he possessed a rare dance talent, mirroring Lord Shiva's divine movements. His being became a vessel for the energies of various deities, embodying the essence of Mother Sakthi and the valour of Subramanyam. When infused with feminine energy, his voice resonated with the softness of a gentle breeze while channelling Subramanyam's spirit, which transformed him into a serpent-like entity, hissing and slithering with divine grace.

Manifestation of Miracles

Swamy stood as a peerless adept in the realm of miracles, performing feats akin to those attributed to Sathya Sai Baba himself. Despite never receiving formal training in the veena, he effortlessly produced melodies that stirred the soul, transcending the boundaries of musical prowess. Often cloistered in a darkened room, assuming yogic postures beyond human endurance, he emitted an aura infused with the fragrances of camphor and sandalwood, symbols of divine presence permeating the mundane.

A Mystic from Birth

Swamy exhibited signs of mysticism that left his parents awestruck even in infancy. A pilgrimage to the Sri Narapura Venkateswara Temple, an ancient Hindu temple *in Jammalamadugu*, YSR Kadapa District, Andhra Pradesh, India. They saw him transfixed by the divine idol of Venkateswara, a moment that foreshadowed the divine mission he was destined to undertake. Born under the auspicious star of Shravana Nakshatra, associated with the lord of the Seven Hills, Swamy's celestial alignment marked him as a chosen vessel of divine grace.

The Unfathomable Nature of Avatara Purushas

While my heart is drawn to the idea of compiling a comprehensive tome chronicling Swamy's divine journey, I am humbled by the realization that the Avatara Purushas transcend mortal interpretation. Their essence defies comprehension, their deeds beyond the grasp of human understanding. Thus, I stand in awe of Swamy's divine presence, content in the knowledge that his legacy shall endure through the annals of time, a testament to the infinite mysteries of the divine.

Divine Presence and Grace

May Srinivasa's auspicious arrival illuminate the world's path with righteousness, showering this age with the divine grace it dearly needs. Indeed, blessed are those who have been touched by Srinivasa's divine play in their lives.

The Divine Manifestation

Srinivasa's mere sight and touch serve as profound atonement for the accumulated sins of lifetimes! His countenance, akin to a blossoming lotus, radiates purity. The resonance of his celestial voice echoes the primordial sound of 'Om'. And his eyes, as pure as Saligrama stones, hold the mysteries of the cosmos.

Reflections of Divine Encounters

Upon introspection, one finds oneself traversing the days spent in the divine presence, each memory shining like stars along the pathway of the mind.

Childhood Insights and Spiritual Awakening

During those days, the younger Sreenivasa Swamy was in the sixth grade, diligently pursuing his studies. Meanwhile, my sister Vasantha would regale us with detailed accounts of the events unfolding at the high school, painting vivid pictures with her words. One day, Swamy remarked to my sister, "Your elder brother is deeply devout, offering prayers to Lord Rama with unwavering faith. However, he remains sceptical until he witnesses miracles first-hand."

Wonder and Skepticism

In the sacred days of youth, as the young Sreenivasa Swamy delved into his studies, my sister Vasantha would enchant us with tales of the high school's bustling life, weaving each detail with the finesse of a master storyteller. Amidst these narratives, Swamy once remarked to my sister, "Your elder brother is deeply devout, offering prayers to Lord Rama with unwavering faith. However, he remains sceptical until he witnesses miracles first-hand."

Navigating the Realm of Miracles

These musings echoed in my mind as I pondered Srinivasa Swamy's divine plays, known for their inexplicable mystique. How do these miracles happen? Despite my upbringing in a remote village, Veparala, and my limited understanding of science, I could not reconcile these wonders with rational explanations. Science, which I had learned about in that humble village, seemed like a journey into the depths of the mind, exploring the mysteries of the universe.

The Midnight Visitor

Srinivasa Swamy was always available whenever we wanted to see him and would spend quality time with all of us. One day, my mother shared a distressing experience with him. She told him that every midnight, a Sadhu, a saint-like figure, would circle her bed three times without causing any physical disturbance but leaving her deeply frightened. This happened repeatedly, and she grew more scared each night, especially when she started hearing loud noises at the backdoor of our compound.

When asked about it, Swamy explained that our house, like the entire colony, was built on a burial ground, and the Sadhu's tomb was beneath our home. Swamy said the Sadhu was seeking salvation or liberation. He stayed with us that night, and at midnight, he rose, went to the door, and spoke in a hushed tone to someone unseen. Later, he assured us that the Sadhu would no longer appear. True to his word, the disturbances ceased from that night onwards.

The Mysterious Bath

Another event that remains vivid in my memory is Swamy's bathing ritual. My mother would always keep a bucketful of hot water and a towel ready for him. Sometimes, he would spend over an hour in the bathroom, and we could continuously hear the sound of water splashing. We often wondered how a single bucket of water could last so long. Later, Swamy revealed to my mother that many saints came to bathe him during this time. These are mysteries that are beyond human comprehension, showcasing the divine connections Swamy maintained.

Foretelling the Future

During the filming of "Lambadolla Ramadas" in and around Mylavaram, the actors, including Chalam, Alluri Rama Lingaiah, Narasimha Raju, and Sathyanarayana, along with the director and the photographer, were staying in a nearby guest room. They visited Swamy at our neighbour's house and were amazed when he accurately described their personal problems and life events. Swamy even predicted the delayed release of the film, and all his predictions came true.

These experiences with Srinivasa Swamy reveal a spiritual realm that intertwines with our everyday lives, offering glimpses of the divine and reminding us of the mysteries beyond human understanding.

Embracing Faith and Belief

Yet, despite my efforts to approach these phenomena with the scepticism of a seasoned scientist or detective, I couldn't deny the certainty that Swami's miracles instilled unwavering faith in his devotees. His suggestions or invisible blessings brought solace and belief to his spiritual kin without question, leaving an indelible mark on their souls.

Divine Decree and Surreal Moments

"Tonight," Swami's voice echoed through the room, "I shall visit your home in the guise of a serpent and partake of the milk and rice." Vasantha stood transfixed, her eyes wide with astonishment at the divine decree. "Even if your brother attempts, he shall not succeed," Swami continued, his words carrying an air of certainty.

Anticipation and Revelation

I rushed to prepare the offerings outside with a sense of urgency and anticipation coursing through my veins. I carefully placed the milk and rice and repeatedly checked, unable to shake off the excitement filling the air.

Divine Call and Spiritual Awakening

As the night wore on, sleep eluded me, and only the intrusion of white ants eventually roused me. The bedclothes clung to my skin, damp with sweat, a testament to the moment's intensity.

In that surreal moment, the miraculous transformation from sleeper to guardian left me spellbound, my mind swirling with wonder and disbelief at the divine power that had unfolded before me.

Sacred Invocation and Profound Realization

The endearing call of "Anna" from Swamy resounded with profound tenderness, touching the depths of my soul and setting ablaze the journey of spiritual awakening within me. It wasn't merely a name; it was a sacred invocation, a celestial melody that stirred the essence of my being and ignited the path of divine realization.

Daily Encounters and Miraculous Acts

The first sight of Srinivasa Swamy amidst the misty morning hues graced the threshold of our home in Mylavaram! Each day, he arrived as a gentle presence, a comforting presence. He would share meals with Mother, forging bonds of affection through every morsel consumed together. The marvel of "wonder" became an integral part of daily life, where intimacy found its place in the realm of the miraculous, philosophy found its essence in the extraordinary, and faith found its completeness in unwavering belief.

Encounters with Divine Wonders

Witnessing the serpents twice, the playful creation of Tirumala Prasad into delectable "laddus" with divine hands, the surreal encounter with the primal serpent Adisesha, the subtle realms traversed by sheer will, the blessed fortune of encountering enlightened souls, the creation and bestowal of divine blossoms, conversing through telepathy, clairvoyance, clairaudience, teleportation, and psychic realms akin to the worship of Ramakrishna Paramahansa, the divine displays akin to those of Sri Sathya Sai, Shiva, and Sundaram - all resonated with humility, simplicity, inexplicability, and boundless compassion.

Auspicious Observances

I am sharing a few more experiences that I encountered with Swamy. On the auspicious Nagula Chavithi, a rare happening I witnessed. It is a Hindu festival celebrated to worship serpent gods. It holds religious significance and is observed in Andhra Pradesh and Karnataka. On this day, people perform puja, offer prayers, and seek blessings from the Nagas. The festival is associated with Lord Shiva, Lord Vishnu, Lord Kartikeya, and Lord Ganesha, who are all linked to snakes. Snake worship is considered important in Hindu culture.

Sacred Encounter with Serpents

My mother had given me a cup of cow milk and asked us to pour it into a snake hole, which we call Nagulaputta', and swami accompanied me. Swamy whispered something near the hole, and suddenly, a big cobra came gently from the hole. Swamy took it to his hand, pampered it like a mother, and later poured it into its mouth. It gently swallowed and disappeared into the hole, leaving a sense of wonder to me. I like seeing snakes and playing with them, and I cannot bear someone beating them. I got the feeling that Swamy was feeding me. I remember Swamy, on a number of occasions, telling me, 'Anna, you are being protected by NAGA DEVATHA invisibly, and you are NAGAMSA, hailing from that family of serpents. Beings of higher awareness or consciousness from different worlds, away from our world and earth, come to assist, and the wise beings of Naga Loka also would help mankind rise to higher awareness.

Reflecting on another profound encounter, my mind drifts to the sacred precincts of the Local Shivalayam Temple in Mylavaram, nestled along the banks of the tranquil river Penna. Within the hallowed confines of this ancient sanctuary, a remarkable incident unfolded, etching itself into the fabric of my memory.

A Startling Provocation

It was a day like any other, filled with the gentle whispers of prayer and the lingering scent of incense. As devotees gathered to pay homage to the divine, a small stone, propelled by the innocence of my brother, Ganesh, found its mark on an unsuspecting inhabitant of the temple. This venerable snake coiled around the revered Shiva Lingam. The serpent, startled and aggrieved by this sudden intrusion, hissed vehemently, its hood raised in a display of defensive fury.

Divine Grace

Amidst the tension that hung in the air, Swamy, guided by a compassion born of divine wisdom, approached the scene. With a voice suffused with tranquillity, he addressed the aggrieved serpent, whispering words of pacification and understanding. "Don't be angry," he gently urged. Ganesha is but a child, unaware of the pain his actions may cause you. Depart from this place in peace."

Miraculous Dissolution

In response to Swamy's soothing entreaty, the snake, as if touched by the divine grace that emanated from his being, acquiesced without hesitation. In a moment of miraculous transformation, the serpent vanished from sight, its departure marking the cessation of conflict and the restoration of harmony within the sacred precincts of the temple.

Reflections on Divine Harmony

This poignant incident serves as a testament to the power of compassion and understanding in fostering harmony between all beings, regardless of form or disposition. Swamy's intervention exemplifies the divine principle of ahimsa, or non-violence, transcending species boundaries and instilling a reverence for all life forms.

Lessons in Compassion

As I reflect on this profound moment, I am reminded of the timeless wisdom encapsulated in Swamy's words and actions. His compassionate approach towards even the most misunderstood of creatures serves as a beacon of light, guiding us towards a deeper understanding of the interconnectedness of all existence.

The Legacy of Divine Harmony

Long after the echoes of this encounter fade into the annals of time, its resonance continues reverberating within my soul's chambers. It stands as a poignant reminder of the transformative power of empathy and understanding, illuminating the path towards a world where compassion reigns supreme, and all beings coexist in perfect harmony.

Journey to the Astral Plane

In the second instance, on the day of Vinayaka Chavithi, Swamy asked me to accompany them, and we went. He patted me, and we disappeared somewhere that looked to me like a different world. The people there were more than six feet, with bigger limbs. I could see water, vegetation and many others. It was a crazy world that I had never seen, and I realized it was not the Earth but the life beyond.

Then, Swamy asked me, 'Anna, keep it yourself; it is a different astral world. I thought of showing it to you, and it is not for publicity. It has some purpose; you don't look back or proceed further without asking anything. I followed him for a while, and suddenly, my so-called rational, I mean my irrational mind, propelled me to look back, and Swamy again patted my back, in a split-second, reached where we started our journey.

He asked me to keep it to myself, but I always habitually shared it with others, especially my mother and brothers, who gazed at me with a sense of wonder. Later, as usual, Maya, the illusion prevails, hiding such rare happenings in life. I remembered Swamy telling me, 'Anna, you will forget what happened, including what you had seen, ' and it happened to me. But certain impressions got imprinted, and they will not escape from my sight.

Divine Insights and Reflections

He shared the accident that my mother had while travelling on a bike that I drove with my sister. I realized that predictions and revealing the events that happened are common and easy for them because they know our past, present, and future.

Teachings and Spiritual Evolution

Swamy, the embodiment of divinity, could facilitate spiritual transformation and bestow inner evolution with mere thought. To such a divine incarnation, I taught a lesson titled "Paravartanam," representing "total internal reflection," a science lesson. It was a profound irony to teach about light to Swamy, who represents the universal rays illuminating our path, dispelling the darkness of doubt and bestowing universal peace. He used to listen to me like a good boy, showing great interest in learning. It was akin to teaching about rays to the sun, the bestower of light.

Divine Encounters: Embracing the Spiritual Essence of Sri Srinivasa Swamy

Initial Devotion and Fear

My brother, Dr. Hari, underwent profound experiences with Sri Srinivasa Swamy. He harboured a fear of God, a phrase familiar to many on their spiritual journeys. Initially, devotion for him meant adorning himself with Vibhoothi or Red Saffron or wearing a dollar, with fear induced by elders overshadowing love for God.

Miraculous Encounters and Deepening Devotion

When Sri Srinivasa Swamy was introduced into our home by our dear Sister Vasanta, it marked a memorable event. My brother, younger than Swamy by a few years, would sometimes shy away from him. Nevertheless, he fondly reminisces about those encounters and shares them whenever Swamy is discussed in our home.

Swamy would often become possessed by divine spirits, offering guidance to others and materializing sacred objects such as idols, ash, Vibhoothi, hand rings, and dollars of deities. These experiences left my brother puzzled at first, but gradually, he developed a deep love for Swamy amidst skepticism and belief from others.

The Power of Intuition and Divine Guidance

One day, my brother's class teacher, Khader, sarcastically questioned Swamy's ability to predict MATKA numbers, a form of gambling wherein betting on a number, and if it clicks, the bettor gets more than what he paid. The next day, Swami was exhibiting miracles, like producing Vibhoothi from his hands, and it irritated the teacher, who tried to beat Swamy with his stick. While making an effort, he could not lift his hand, and for a while, he was helpless. Later, he dropped the idea, fearing something odd would happen to him. This led to a confrontation where Swamy's power prevented Khader from causing harm, ultimately leading to reconciliation.

A day later, as my brother journeyed to high school in Veparala, a familiar office subordinate approached him, seeking a Matka number. This individual, known to our family, seemed earnest in their request. My brother, recalling the term from his teacher's sarcastic remark, briefly pondered before tapping into a deeper sense of intuition. Drawing from a sense of spiritual guidance, he thought of Swamy, feeling a subtle pressure to respond. In a moment of spontaneity, he uttered the number 27, guided by a sense that it held significance, perhaps linked to a date. To his astonishment, his suggested number proved auspicious, resulting in a windfall of Rs—100 for the individual's modest investment.

Overwhelmed by the unexpected gain, the office subordinate hurried to my brother, sharing the news with joy and regret, lamenting that they hadn't invested more to reap greater rewards. However, my brother, humbly acknowledging the limitations of his knowledge and the unpredictable nature of such phenomena, confessed his inability to provide another number when asked the following day.

Transformative Love and Joyful Solidarity

Such occurrences transcend mere chance, offering glimpses of a deeper, mysterious order to the universe. They remind us of the interconnectedness of all things and the existence of forces beyond our comprehension. In these moments, we are reminded to trust intuition, listen to the whispers of the divine, and remain open to the possibility of miracles in our lives.

Despite Swamy's humble attire of Nickers adorned with sharp thorns, my brother would playfully tease him, fostering an atmosphere of joy and camaraderie.

During moments of fatigue, Swamy would rest on my mother's lap, and my brother would lovingly embrace his holy feet, finding solace and joy in Swamy's presence. The fear in my brother's heart transformed into unconditional love, as Swamy affectionately called him HARANNA, signifying a timeless bond that transcended lifetimes.

My younger brother, Ganesh, was a little naughty and very pretty, and one day, he rejected eating food when his mother served it with her hands. He was too young, might be less than ten years old. My mother got irritated, and she beat my brother and forced him to eat the food.

While forcibly putting a handful of food into my brother's little mouth, Swami took that piece of food from my mother and put it back into my mother's mouth, converting it into a handful of camphor balls. All of us were shocked and smiled later. Swamy's love for my brother was also beyond words; he used to call Ganesh affectionately.

Divine Visitations and Miracles

Swamy visited our home on I Road on the Thulasi Pooja, a day on which we especially worship Mother Tulasi, who is known for her sanctity. He spent almost an hour speaking to gods in our home, including Sri Sathya Sai Baba. He was laughing, murmuring, and the language of it we hardly deciphered. Swamy often spent time in a dark room praying to Mother Sakthi. Despite the normal circumstances where one's body would be drenched in sweat, hardly any perspiration was noticed on Swamy.

Suddenly, my mother gave him a cup of milk, and he held it with his hands. Within a fraction, he returned it, and the glass didn't touch his lips, but there were no traces of milk. He took leave from us, and while moving, we all noticed camphor pieces falling from his foot. The fragrance from his body was mystifying, like camphor mixed with sandalwood.

My brother accompanied Swamy to Tadipatri in a jeep, and suddenly he used to cry out, "*Anna! Have the Darshan of Sarpa Devatha.*" When he makes his journey, many angles escort him. Suddenly the headlights of the jeep failed, and it was complete darkness. It was a ghat section, and the driver got scared driving in darkness. However, Swamy said, "*Go slowly and no vehicles will come in the opposite direction till you reach the main road.*" The same thing happened. If we recall such incidents, we get goosebumps now, but at that point in time, it was considered casual due to the impact of Maya.

He used to possess different deities during his childhood. On a particular day, there were devotees waiting for his Darshan. He was hardly 13 years old when that incident happened. Suddenly Swamy was hissing like a cobra and simply crawled throughout the room, and the persons present were scared. The eyes were different, and the voice, which used to be gentle, got ferocious. Likewise, we had seen Swamy possessing divine spirits, and he was unable to prevent such divine possessions which were beyond his control at that point in time. These look like imaginative stories, but they are facts beyond doubt, for they are witnessed with our naked eye.

Seeking Solace and Finding Miracles

The colony residents, their friends, and their relatives would often seek solace in Swamy's presence, confiding in him their troubles, finding comfort in his soothing words and hopeful solutions.

My brother, immersed in love for Swamy, found immense pleasure in his presence, oblivious to worldly troubles. Our home, adorned with images and idols of various deities, witnessed Swamy's communion with them, a sight perceived as eccentric by some yet profound and wondrous to us.

One day, Swamy was seen at our neighbour's verandah, where a miraculous Laddu appeared, reminiscent of the offerings from the Lord of Seven Hills. Such miracles were abundant, from objects disappearing instantly to divine manifestations, leaving us in awe and reverence.

On one festival day, I believe the festival of Thulasi Mata, Swamy asked my mother to prepare Kesari Bath, a sweet item. She did it and put it in a closed steel box. Later, after a while, he asked her to open it, and there was no Prasadam kept in the box. It disappeared, and there was no trace of it. It was like a washed vessel.

My brother, Dr. Hari, escaped getting drowned in Penna waters while going to college, and Swamy was staying in our home, telling my parents about it. They were shocked, waiting for him. They offered prayers to Goddess Gangamma, and the same night, they went to the Penna River, which was overflowing and causing loud sounds. There were countless miracles; all of them need space, and it is enough to have space for him in our hearts.

The Divine Presence in Everyday Life

My father got transferred to Anantapur. As there was no house, they dropped their luggage in the room I rented for studying for a B.Sc. in Government Arts College. One of my father's colleagues and our neighbor could search for a nice house within a day, while my parents were moving around the locality to get a house for less than Rs. 100 because of my father's meager salary, and he was due for retirement shortly.

My mother found a house on the next street, but the owners happened to be our distant relatives. When approached, the owner's wife said it was given to others. It was false; she suspected that with four children and an aged grandmother, we would not pay them rent. The owner, a retired Tahsildar, showed consideration, which was rejected.

Later, Swamy told my mother that they were telling lies and did not give the house to anyone. He had given Akshintalu (rice coloured with turmeric, oil, and red saffron) after prayer and asked my mother to throw

Divine Encounters with Ganapathi Sachidananda Swamy

A Journey of Profound Spiritual Experiences and Divine Guidance

My journey with Ganapathi Sachidananda Swamy of Mysore has been a rollercoaster of profound spiritual experiences and divine guidance. One such life-altering moment occurred during Swamiji's visit to His Ashram at Anantapur. As I found myself in His divine presence at the Datta Mandir, I was not just overwhelmed but completely swept away by an indescribable surge of emotions, a feeling that transcended words. This inexplicable and unspoken inspiration propelled me to compose the divine hymn "DATTAPADI."

Presenting "DATTAPADI" to Swamiji

Overcoming my initial fear, I decided to share my creation, "DATTAPADI," with Swamiji. I entrusted this task to Venu Gopal, a family friend and a devout follower of Swamiji. Venu's journey from a place of doubt and skepticism to one of unwavering faith in Swamiji is a testament to the transformative power of devotion and belief. His courage to speak up when Swamiji inquired about our well-being is a story that not only inspires but also reassures us that faith can indeed move mountains.

With a trembling voice, Venu conveyed that the "DATTAPADI" was an offering from Dr. Nagaraj. He further said, "Swamiji, when you visited Datta Mandir in Anantapur, Dr. Nagaraj had your Darshan. When Sri Swamiji graced the devotees at Datta mandir recently, Dr Nagaraj, upon being gazed at by Swamiji's divine eyes, experienced an electrifying transcendence. Guided by this intuitive, unlettered inspiration, he composed these divine hymns."

In response, Swamiji asked Venu, "How are they? Meaning our home, which we call Kovela." With a feeble voice, Venu said, "They are okay with your blessings." Swamiji instructed Venu, "Tell loudly that all is well, all should be well, and there should be global peace."

Inferring the Spiritual Message

The spiritual message in this encounter is profound. Swamiji's inquiry and subsequent instruction underscore the importance of expressing and affirming positivity and well-being. Swamiji underscores the power of spoken words and intentions by inquiring about the well-being of our home and insisting that Venu speak loudly. The directive for global peace, a call that transcends personal boundaries and encompasses all welfare, is a powerful reminder of the universal nature of spirituality. Swamiji's actions and words inspire us to recognize our blessings, express gratitude, and foster a mindset of peace and harmony that extends beyond personal spheres to embrace the entire world.

Swamiji's Blessings and Benedictory Message

Venu handed over the consecrated booklet containing the DATTAPADI booklet to his holiness Swamiji. Swamiji fixed His gaze on "Tasmai Sri Guravenamaha" and studied it with transcendental concentration. Swamiji then took "DATTAPADI" into His divine hands, rubbing it as if nestling and caressing His son Nagaraj in the protective lap of divine hands.

Swamiji then placed His forefinger on the title "DATTAPADI" and chanted entrancingly: "DATTA." At that moment, it felt as if Lord Sri Dattatreya Himself appeared before Swamiji.

Later, Swamiji conveyed a benedictory message through Venu: "Tell him that Swamiji is omniscient;

He knows everything. Also, tell him that Swamiji has read it completely. Everyone should read it. Give it to Kuppa Krishnamurthy (the biographer of Sachidananda's Dattacharitra, a thousand-two-hundred-page biography on Swamiji), and it has to be printed in Bhaktimala."

A Personal Encounter in Hyderabad

I recall another profound experience when I met Swamiji in Hyderabad. Innocently, I asked, "Swamy, give me Pada Namaskaram." Swamiji immediately said, "NO." He explained that everything was given to me in previous lives and nothing was needed now. Although initially disturbed by His response, I later went into deep contemplation. To my wonder, I observed Swamiji standing next to me, smiling beautifully. He signalled me to take Pada Namaskara and blessed me.

Divine Wisdom and Human Limits: The Journey of Faith

This experience taught me that divine ways are mysterious. Just as a mother sometimes shows anger but holds immense love, God's ways can be difficult to interpret. A mother may gently reprimand a child but later hug and kiss them with love. Similarly, Swamiji's ways are filled with profound love and blessings, even if they are not immediately understood.

We should not claim to understand God; our complex mindsets make this impossible. Instead, we should accept God's love. Why waste time counting the fruits on a mango tree? Instead, we should take a ripened one, enjoy it, and express gratitude for the fruit it shared, which it never consumes itself.

The divine experiences and Ganapathi Sachidananda Swamy's blessings have immeasurably enriched my spiritual life. His ways may be beyond our understanding, but accepting His love and guidance brings profound peace and joy.

The Divine Power of a Smile: Embracing the Essence of Life

In the grand tapestry of existence, we often overlook one of the simplest yet most profound gifts bestowed upon us – the smile. *Many of us know the saying: "A smile costs nothing but makes life worth it!"* Yet, how often do we truly smile, even for a fleeting moment, to illuminate our faces and the world around us?

Is it hard to smile? If not, why do we see so few smiles in our daily lives?

A smile is an ambrosial elixir, a divine nectar that nourishes the soul and brings the essence of life to the forefront. It is an evangelic ecstasy, lifting our spirits to celestial heights. This simple gesture holds potent medicine for the ailments of the body, mind, and soul. It is an antidote for anger and hatred, transforming negativity into positivity.

A smile is not just a social or cosmetic expression; it is a cosmic connection. Smiles born from tears are the most fertile, watering the seeds of compassion and empathy. A true smile is innocent, truthful, cheerful, faithful, selfless, and fearless, embodying the purest virtues.

Smiling boosts our immunity, not only physical but spiritual. It pleases the Divine, inviting grace and blessings into our lives. A smile deals with life's challenges, feels deeply within, and heals wounds unseen.

A smile is light, illuminating our path. It is life, breathing vitality into our existence. A smile sparkles, adding brilliance to our journey. It stands as an emblem of purity and peace, reflecting the divine essence within us.

Consider the flowers through which God smiles. These blossoms live for the day, smiling throughout their brief existence, teaching us a profound lesson:

"O! Man! Look at us! We live for the day. We smile throughout the day. Think for a while, why don't you smile?!"

Embrace the divine power of a smile. It is the essence of life, a beacon of hope, and a reflection of our inner light. Let it be your spiritual practice, your daily offering to the world. In every smile, feel the touch of the Divine, and share this sacred gift generously.

Life is fleeting, but the impact of a smile endures. It transcends boundaries, heals divisions, and brings us closer to the divine truth that we are all interconnected. So, smile more often, for in each smile lies the power to transform the world.

SMILE!

Many know: "A smile costs nothing but makes life worth it!"

How many really throw a smile, even for a while, that lights up their face to glow?

Is it hard to smile?!

Then why do people hardly smile?

A smile is an ambrosial elixir.

A smile is an evangelic ecstasy of the soul.

A smile is a potent medicine for the diseases of body, mind, and soul.

A smile is an antidote to anger and hatred.

A smile is not merely social and cosmetic;

A smile is essentially cosmic.

Smiles rooted in tears are the most fertile smiles.

A true smile is always innocent, truthful, cheerful, faithful, selfless, and fearless.

A smile boosts immunity,

Pleases God and begets the grace of divinity.

A smile deals,

A smile feels,

A smile heals.

A smile is light,

A smile is life.

A smile sparkles life.

A smile is an emblem of purity and peace.

God smiles through flowers, and smiling flowers
exclaim:

"O! Man! Look at us!

We live for the day,

We smile throughout the day.

Think for a while,

Why don't you smile?!"

A Cry for Divine Intervention: A Spiritual Plea to Sai Baba

Cosmic Indifference

Baba! Your Holiness, I have been a vessel of unrelenting torment since my earliest memories. Every moment of my excruciating agony is known to you, yet the cosmos remains indifferent. The weight of my suffering is unbearable, Baba, and I am desperate for your intervention. Why, Baba, why?

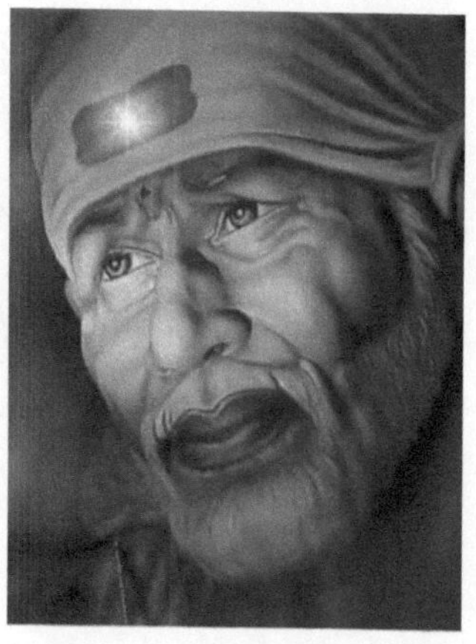

The Depths of Suffering

My mind is a battlefield of pain, scarred and ulcerated. The night is a terror, and the morning is a chorus of groans. Each day is a shapeless mass of clay moulded by the weight of my suffering. My inner light, my Tejas, is trapped in the Muladhara, and the knots of my unresolved past strangle my spirit!

Divine Will

Baba, from the moment of my birth, your divine will has guided every step I've taken. Yet, this relentless cycle of life and death has worn my patience threadbare. Your indifference, Baba, deepens my wounds and pushes me closer to the edge of despair. But I still hold on to the hope of your divine intervention, for I believe in your power to bring spiritual enlightenment. Why, then, is this delay in your divine intervention?

Awaken Sai Consciousness

Having no other refuge, I have earnestly sought shelter at your lotus feet. "The infinite soul, Baba, is by your side," the divine words of Bhagwan Sri Ram SIR, spoken truthfully, infuse life into me like the elixir of life in my final breath, Baba!

If it is true that you, the epitome of compassion and extraordinary mercy, will protect me under the wings of your merciful glance, then why should I, who have no other support, still endure this excruciating torment? Baba, I am clinging to the hope of your divine intervention, for without it, my existence feels like a deadly poison to me.

Oh, Lord Sai Nath, I am but an orphan in this vast universe. I am unable to transform my heart into a sanctuary of peace through my efforts to summon you with my spiritual strength to reside within me. Without you, I am a burden to myself, consumed by unbearable agony. My very existence feels like a deadly poison. I am unworthy of your full mercy, yet I cannot fathom a life without it. Why, then, should I continue to live...? How can I bear to live distanced from your divine grace? I long for your presence, Baba, and I depend on your mercy.

Drained Vital Energy

The constant assaults on my sensitive spirit have drained my vital energy and Atmic spirit. Living with the agony of life and death is like a poison churning my being. 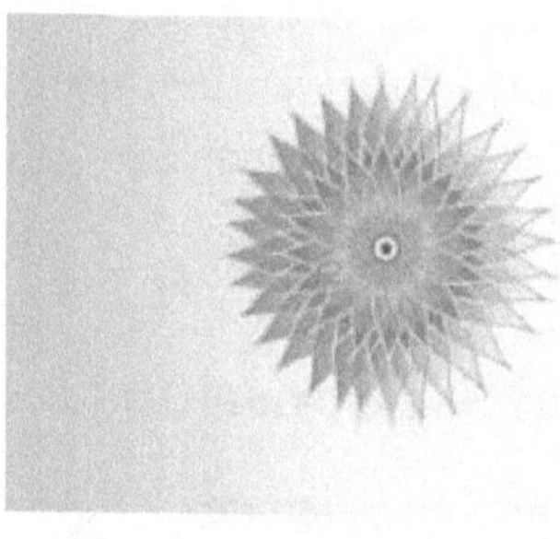 You, with a poison-filled throat and a gentle heart, please look at my life's turmoil with your inner eye. Witness my existence crying out in agony. Does my cry not melt your heart? My deathly lamentation, which can shake the heavens, does it not reach your compassionate heart, Sai?

Silent Agony

When time, like a sadist, delights in my suffering, are you silent and indifferent? Time, the punisher seems to have forgotten its limits and boundaries. Do not let this cruel magic continue, Sai. Isn't Dwarka Mai, your divine wish-fulfilling tree, beyond time?

Compassionate Healing

Every cell of mine cannot bear the wound, distant from your compassionate healing. If my life's thread snaps under the weight of this suffering, time, the punisher, will ignite my pyre. Will you protect me from the demonic actions of time and punish the evil planets? Will you come to save me, Sai Deva?

New Year's Wishes

I wish to welcome the new year with the mantra flowers and offer the auspicious aarti with the self-light of the soul. Gathering all powers, I offered Bilva leaves at your lotus feet and gave you the Neerajan. Yet, your divine incidents struck my spirit like thunderbolts, withering me in pain. Only with great joy did my vital forces endure your indifference, sustaining my existence. Parashakti knows! Baba knows! Lord Sri Ram knows!

Bhagwan Sri Ram Sir told me,

- ✼ "Nagaraj! The divine arrow you have unleashed will pierce through obstacles and reach its target," said Baba. All divine power is in your back. Hereafter, you will face no more difficulties. Baba's invisible helping hands are protecting you. You will attain what you desire and become what you aspire to be. What you receive is the essence of your dreams. God never deceives you. Just have a little more patience.

- ✼ Your 'regret' about your unalterable 'past', 'dread' about an ambiguous future' and uncertainty about the un-understandable 'present' — will soon dissolve into the bewitching embrace of beaming smiles. The day when fortune smiles on you is not far off. Don't worry. Begin your disinterested discharge of duty. March ahead! Onward, forward, Godward!!!

א   In the subterranean caves of your life, there are meditating monks; their boiling belly bears Divine Embryo. Calmly bear the birth pangs. The birth of mirth is not far off.

א   What if there is a penetrating, outrageous storm outside? There are outstretched protecting arms of God beside!!! It's only God who does not deceive you; it is only God who does not pay a deaf year to your demands. So don't doubt Him: Believe in Him and Be patient and you will be what you want to be!!! Be a paragon of placid mind, embodiment of endurance, established in unperturbable Self.

If this grace is withheld even in this heart-wrenching and critical phase of my existence, I shall forcibly sever the thread of my life on the fragrance of Shirdi Sai's essence. I will release my physical form into the subtle or astral realm!

Surviving Adversities

Barely breathing under the adversities caused by the negative planetary forces in childhood, I have not fully recovered from setbacks that shattered my sadhana. Bhagwan Sri Ram SIR's divine, handwritten letters keep me alive, promising divine protection and fulfilment. Yet, if grace eludes me in this critical phase, I will sever my life thread, seeking liberation in the subtle or astral sphere.

A Plea for Rescue: Before My Life Unravels

Before my forbearance is shattered into pieces, before my accumulated frustrations unleash volcanic, violent agitations, before my heart's thudding pounding ceases, before my life veins rupture and bleed through mouth, nostrils, and eyes, before my life thread strains, before I take my last breath, and before my yearning existence collapses... Kindly rescue me, my Baba, the saviour of my life."

Seeking Liberation

If that moment arrives, the compassionate primordial power, the supreme 'Kali' mother, will hear my cries and save me, granting liberation. Revive my life with compassion if your heart is softer than ice. Protect me, Sai. You are the wish-fulfilling tree, Dwarkamai. Before my endurance shatters, save me, my Baba, the saviour of my life.

Desire to Live

I wish to live like Shiva, Bhagavan! Protect my flickering life lamp with the oil of compassion. Grant me complete life consciousness attainment. Protect me, and let me reach your supreme abode. Please take me to your divine feet!

Knowledge of Brahman

Is attaining the supreme knowledge of Brahman harder than achieving the highest in medical science? Though you grant time, your indifference prevents the rain of compassion, wounding me at every step. I am caught in the whirlpool of worldly turmoil, choked by satanic Maya.

Twisted Life Thread

Delusions, fears, anxieties, and psychic tortures have twisted and strained my life thread. Death is preferable to this deathly state. Lord Sri Ram's bestowed Sri Sai Salagrama supports my life, healing my heart's wildfire.

Bhagwan Sri Ram's "SIR" materialization of Sri Sai Salagrama is my life support, inspiring me as the soul and essence of the universe. It rejuvenates with devotion, offering solace to burning volcanoes within my heart and a panacea for healing the wounds of body, mind and soul.

He materialized it from the prasadam (LADDU) at PUTTAPARTHY. It really restored me as a revitalizing tonic. I believed that you were weaving the threads of my destiny. The words of Bhagwan Sri Ram, '*Nagaraj, God had so little love for others that He did not allow them to suffer. He made others temporarily happy, but they were permanently unhappy. God loves you so much that He wants to make you happy. He made you temporarily unhappy only to make you permanently happy*' again restored my sapped-out energies.

However, my heart cries that your complete compassion and grace have not manifested for me. Despair, indifference, disappointment, and humility have consumed the sun of my heart.

Cosmic Grace

Baba! The torment of an ailing heart awaits your cosmic grace. Your indifference wounds me deeply. I can no longer bear this, my Baba. Save me!

Longing for Kailasa

"O Parameshwara! How many lifetimes have passed since I last visited Kailash? Will I ever have the chance to behold it again?

I yearn to behold my Mother Bramaramba. With these very eyes, I long to see my divine parents. I wish to rest ly on my mother's lap, forgetting the world as I sleep peacefully. The mere thought of sharing small morsels of food with my mother fills my heart with joy.

In the divine presence of Lord Shiva and Parvati, may I be blessed with the radiance of divine light, wisdom, profound meditation, and the blossoming passion of a flower? Bless me, Father, with your grace and guidance so that I may embody the fervour and dedication of this divine flower, spreading its fragrance of devotion and love in all aspects of my life. May I walk the path of righteousness and spiritual growth, guided by your divine presence, and may my passion for truth and enlightenment shine brightly for all eternity.

A Divine Presence in the Temple Home

In this sacred temple, parents eagerly call out, "Sri Ram, Sai Ram," hoping to glimpse your divine form. They listen to the tales of your miraculous deeds, meditating upon you, worshipping you, and waiting for your grace, oh Father!

- **Hari's Earnest Prayer**: Our younger brother Hari, burdened and weary, drags his days along. His tired heart constantly echoes with the name "Sai." With tearful eyes filled with longing, he waits for your mercy. Inwardly focused, he constantly seeks your protection and prays with a heart full of surrender, seeking your compassionate love.

- **Ganesh's Spiritual Immersion**: The youngest brother, Ganesh, is absorbed in the wealth of inner meditation. He is immersed in the contemplation of Sri Ram and Sai, resonating with the divine consciousness of "Sri Ram" and "Sai."

- **Sai Nivedita's Silent Devotion**: Our sister, Sai Nivedita, undergoes soul purification. In her deep sleep, she envisions you, remaining silent and humble. With pure thoughts, she prays to you, her beloved deity, for the creation of nurturing love.

Within this divine sanctuary, each family member finds solace and strength in their unique way. They unite in their devotion to you, seeking your grace, love, and guidance. Your presence, dear Father, is the light that guides their hearts, filling their lives with hope and divine blessings.

Sacred Invocation: A Prayer for Healing and Enlightenment"

"Baba! Heal my traumatized life. Consecrate the deeply wounded layers of my subconscious. Reanimate me. Rejuvenate me. Infuse cosmic light into the very essence of my being! Guide my spiritual practice. Bless me with academic brilliance, professional success, and spiritual enlightenment.

Granting Benedictions for Complete Life's Spiritual Attainment: In resonance with the soul's essence, may your divine presence forever illuminate our path.

Awakening Divine Compassion: Reflections from My Spiritual Journey

In the quiet depths of my inner journey, I have discovered profound teachings that resonate deeply with the essence of divine compassion. This spiritual exploration has illuminated my path, guiding me towards a deeper understanding of universal truths and nurturing a sense of empathy and kindness within me.

Embracing Selfless Sacrifice and Patience

As I journey toward spiritual maturity, I appreciate the transformative power of selfless sacrifice and patience. Letting go of ego-driven desires and embracing a purpose greater than myself has opened my heart to a profound connection with others. Patience has become not just a virtue but a practice—an essential companion on my journey towards spiritual maturity and inner peace.

Finding Sanctuary in Compassion

Amidst life's challenges and uncertainties, I have found solace in the sanctuary of compassion. This nurturing presence, embodying the essence of divine love, heals wounds and soothes troubled souls. It transcends boundaries of culture and creed, offering a universal balm for humanity's collective heartaches. Through quiet reflection and heartfelt empathy, I have witnessed the profound impact of compassion in uplifting spirits and fostering resilience.

Nurturing Through Generous Giving

Compassionate giving has become a cornerstone of my spiritual practice. It is not merely about material offerings but about extending a compassionate hand, offering understanding, and sharing kindness without expectation. In these acts, I have discovered the joy of selfless service and the profound interconnectedness that binds us all. Each gesture of kindness becomes a testament to the transformative power of compassion in enriching lives and fostering a sense of community.

Embodying Divine Virtue and Mercy

Virtue and mercy, fundamental to spiritual teachings, have guided my actions and shaped my character. They have taught me to embrace ethical conduct and compassionately navigate the complexities of human relationships. By embodying these divine qualities, I strive to contribute positively to the world around me, cultivating harmony and goodwill in every interaction.

Seeking Guidance in Divine Light

In moments of doubt and confusion, I turn to the guiding light of spiritual wisdom. I connect with the divine presence within and around me through prayer, meditation, and introspection. This spiritual connection offers clarity amidst life's challenges and strengthens my resolve to walk my path with faith and courage. It reminds me that divine grace is ever-present in every trial and triumph, guiding me towards greater understanding and spiritual fulfilment.

Transcending Fear Through Spiritual Awakening

Fear has often been a barrier on my spiritual journey, clouding my vision and hindering my growth. Yet, I have learned to transcend fear through spiritual awakening and deepening connection with the divine. I embrace each moment with trust and surrender, knowing that divine compassion surrounds me, offering protection and peace. This inner transformation has liberated me from fear, empowering me to embrace life's uncertainties with grace and resilience.

Conclusion: A Journey Towards Compassionate Living

My inner journey towards awakening divine compassion has been transformative. It has shaped my perspective and nurtured a profound empathy and kindness. As I continue to walk this path, I am inspired to embody these teachings in every aspect of my life, fostering a more compassionate and harmonious world. May my reflections serve as a beacon of hope and inspiration for others on their spiritual journeys, guiding them towards greater love, understanding, and enlightenment.

Child Ways

My sister, Sai Nivedita, shared a piece of her poetry, "Child Ways," with Bhagwan Sri Ram. I felt inspired to share it along with the inferences I drew for my own learning.

In my silence
There is eloquence
Will you hear it?
In your silence
There is silencer
Will you speak to me?
In my smiles
There are tears
Do you feel them?
In your smile
There are pearls

Will you give them to me?

In my love

There is an 'orphan'

Will you patronize me?

In your love

There lies Blessing...

Will you confer it on me?

Can a beggar be so bold?

I stand at thy threshold.

Don't turn wild

Am I not your child?

Kindly give me

Alms of grace

In thy Heart

Bestow me a place.

'He is your saviour

My conscience' says.,

May my life

Rest in peace.

Embracing the Silence: A Journey of Spiritual Yearning

"Child Ways" is a deeply evocative poem that opens the door to a profound spiritual dialogue between the seeker and the divine. It reflects an intimate yearning for connection, understanding, and acceptance, revealing the raw emotions and vulnerabilities inherent in the human quest for spiritual fulfilment. Through its verses, the poem guides us on a journey of silent eloquence, emotional duality, and bold supplication, ultimately leading to a plea for divine grace and peace.

The Eloquent Silence

"In my silence, there is eloquence." These opening lines capture the essence of a spiritual truth: silence is not an absence but a presence. In the stillness of our hearts and minds, there is a depth of feeling and thought that words often fail to convey. This eloquence of silence is a sacred language, a way in which the soul communicates its deepest desires and yearnings to the divine. It is a reminder that our quiet moments are filled with meaning, and within them lies the potential for profound spiritual connection. As Rumi beautifully said, "Silence is the language of God; all else is poor translation." This silence allows us to tune into the divine frequency, where we can find clarity, guidance, and peace.

The Divine Silence

"In your silence, There is a silencer." This line speaks to a common spiritual struggle: the perceived silence of the divine. When faced with life's challenges and the soul's urgent pleas, the absence of a clear response from the divine can feel like a heavy silence, a silencer that deepens our sense of isolation. Yet, this divine silence is not a void but a space for trust and faith. It invites us to listen more deeply, to attune our hearts to the subtle whispers of divine presence and guidance that often go unnoticed. As Mother Teresa once expressed, "In the silence of the heart, God speaks. If you face God in prayer and silence, God will speak to you." This divine silence is a sacred invitation to deepen our faith, to trust in the unseen, and to find solace in the quiet assurance of God's presence.

The Duality of Emotions

"In my smiles, there are tears." This poignant line captures the complexity of human emotions, where joy and sorrow coexist. Our outward expressions of happiness can mask inner struggles and pain, a duality that speaks to the heart of the human experience. The divine, in its infinite compassion, understands this complexity and invites us to bring all of our emotions to the sacred relationship. "In your smile, there are pearls" symbolizes the purity and beauty of divine grace. These pearls of wisdom and compassion are the gifts that the divine bestows upon us, inviting us to embrace both our joy and our sorrow. As Khalil Gibran wrote, "The deeper that sorrow carves into your being, the more joy you can contain." The divine smile, radiant with grace, assures us that our tears are seen, our pains are understood, and our joys are celebrated.

The Longing for Divine Love

"In my love, there is an 'orphan'" reveals a deep sense of spiritual orphanhood, a feeling of being lost and yearning for the nurturing presence of the divine. This metaphor of orphanhood captures the essence of our spiritual quest: the longing to be found, to be held, and to be loved unconditionally. In contrast, "In your love, there lies Blessing" speaks to the fullness and completeness of divine love. It is a love that heals, nurtures, and blesses, offering us the assurance that we are never truly alone. As Augustine of Hippo beautifully put it, "Thou hast made us for thyself, O Lord, and our heart is restless until it finds its rest in thee." This divine love is an all-encompassing embrace, a sanctuary where our restless hearts find their true home.

The Boldness of the Seeker

"Can a beggar be so bold... I stand at thy threshold." The metaphor of a beggar at the threshold beautifully illustrates the humility and audacity of the spiritual seeker. In our quest for divine connection, we stand vulnerably at the edge, hoping for acceptance and grace. This boldness is not arrogance but a deep-seated belief in the divine's boundless mercy. "Don't turn wild. Am I not your child?" This heartfelt plea is a reminder of our inherent belonging to the divine. As children of the sacred, we have the right to seek, ask, and hope for divine favour. Julian of Norwich encapsulated this sentiment, "All shall be well, and all shall be well, and all manner of thing shall be well." This boldness is an act of faith, a trust that the divine heart is open and welcoming, ready to bestow grace upon the earnest seeker.

The Alms of Grace

"Kindly give me Alms of grace; in thy Heart, Bestow me a place." These lines encapsulate the ultimate desire of the spiritual seeker: to find a place in the heart of the divine. The alms of grace are not material but spiritual blessings that nourish the soul. To be bestowed a place in the divine heart is to find refuge, acceptance, and peace. It is the culmination of our spiritual journey, where we find rest in the divine embrace. As the Psalmist wrote, "For you, Lord, have never forsaken those who seek you" (Psalm 9:10). This sacred place in the divine heart is our true home, a sanctuary of unconditional love and boundless grace.

The Conscience and Salvation

"'He is your saviour, My conscience' says." This declaration reaffirms the seeker's faith and trust in the divine. It is a call to listen to the inner voice of conscience that guides us towards the sacred. The final wish, "May my life Rest in peace," is a surrender to the divine will, a hope that our spiritual journey will lead us to peace and fulfilment. As Saint Augustine prayed, "You have made us for yourself, O Lord and our heart is restless until it rests in you." This is the ultimate surrender, a trust that our lives, guided by divine love and grace, will find their peace in the sacred.

Conclusion

"Child Ways" is more than a poem; it is a spiritual exploration that invites us to embrace our journey with humility, boldness, and faith. It speaks to the universal human experience of seeking connection with the divine, highlighting the eloquence in our silence, the complexity of our emotions, and the deep yearning for divine love and grace. As we stand at the threshold of the sacred, let us remember that our bold supplications are heard, our tears are seen, and our longing for a place in the divine heart will be met with the boundless compassion and grace of the divine. In the words of Rumi, "What you seek is seeking you." Let us embark on this journey with trust, knowing that the divine heart is always open, ready to receive us, and bestow upon us the alms of grace we so deeply desire.

Finding Serenity Amidst Turmoil

Peace can be found even in the smallest of lamps. It signifies that tranquillity and solace can be discovered in the simplest and most humble places or things. Just as a small lamp can provide light in the darkness, small acts of kindness, moments of reflection, or simple sources of comfort can bring peace and calm to our lives amidst chaos and turmoil. It emphasizes that we don't always need grand gestures or significant changes to find peace; sometimes, it's the little things that can make the most profound difference.

Yet, chaos, unrest, and sorrow sometimes dominate our lives, engulfing our sacred spaces with waves of despair. In moments of profound sorrow, we wonder how we will endure the next minute, hour, or day. During such trying times, the struggles faced by our parents become particularly poignant. Our parents, revered as living deities, bear their own burdens, and in recognizing their struggles, we often find a sense of deep spiritual satisfaction.

Shirdi Baba's profound compassion is a beacon of hope. He embraced those who came to him, treating them with unparalleled love and understanding. He nurtured relationships with immense affection, demonstrating divine parental care. This cosmic connection, the sense of oneness with our parents, transcends the physical and becomes a spiritual bond that offers solace in times of distress.

Life often becomes monotonous, moving from morning to afternoon, evening, and night in a seemingly endless cycle. The routine, the unresolved crises, and the constant friction can erode our patience and sanity. Amidst the clamour of the world, our hearts burn with the longing for peace, making it feel like we are living on the edge of a profound existential crisis.

The societal chaos and the increasing insecurity we face can feel overwhelming. Yet, in the heart of our sacred spaces, the divine truth resonates, reminding us of the ultimate protector, the supreme Lord. We connect with the divine through serving others, experiencing both sorrow and joy as part of a greater cosmic plan.

Even as I recount my journey from childhood trauma to the present moment, the pain inflicted by life's harshness remains vivid. The wounds from my past bleed into my present, making every second a struggle. Despite witnessing my sufferings, my parents remained passive, as if I were an orphan. This profound sense of abandonment has only deepened my quest for divine intervention.

My parents, my Baba, and my cosmic siblings all hold immense significance in my life. Their indifference, however, has sometimes felt like a harsh cosmic joke, leaving me feeling abandoned in my darkest hours. Yet, it is their teachings, their love, and their spiritual presence that have kept me going, even when life seemed unbearably cruel.

The relentless trials and tribulations I faced from a young age have left me scarred but not broken. Despite the ongoing battle with my subconscious demons and the physical and emotional scars, I cling to the hope of divine mercy. My soul cries out for the comforting embrace of the divine, seeking solace and strength to continue my journey.

I find myself praying fervently for rejuvenation, for divine grace to heal my wounds and rekindle my spirit. The cosmic love, the divine guidance, and the promise of an absolute, complete life keep me anchored. I implore the divine to nestle me in its protective arms, transcend my pain, and enlighten my path.

Through all the anguish and adversity, I remain steadfast in my faith, believing that the divine will ultimately guide me to a place of peace and fulfilment. My heart and soul burn with the hope that one day, I will be free from the torment that has plagued my existence, finding serenity in the divine embrace.

In the face of overwhelming despair, I believe that divine compassion will prevail. In its infinite mercy, the supreme power will rescue me from the depths of my suffering, granting me the peace and fulfilment that my soul so desperately seeks.

Universal Prayers

The Glory of Shirdi Sai Baba

Let us celebrate the glory of Shirdi Sai Baba while offering a universal prayer for guidance and protection.

Divine Light, Guide Our Path

Oh, Divine Light, source of wisdom and compassion, Baba,

Our meditation and hearts revolve around you.

You illuminate our souls, melting away sorrows like winter's thaw.

Your presence, like the rising sun, dispels the darkness of ignorance.

The Beacon of Meditation

"You look to me, I look to you." – Sai Satcharitra, Chapter 13

You are the beacon guiding our meditation,

The inner voice of our consciousness.

In you, we find solace and strength,

For you are the sustainer of our spirits, the divine protector.

Seeking Your Mercy

"I am ever living to help and guide all who come to me, who surrender to me and who seek refuge in me." – Sai Satcharitra, Chapter 15

We seek your mercy in times of turmoil, Baba,

For you are the embodiment of love and compassion.

Shield us from the storms of life,

And help us navigate through the trials and tribulations we face.

Illuminating the Soul

"Trust in me, and your prayer shall be answered." – Sai Satcharitra, Chapter 11

Your light reveals the path of righteousness,

Guiding us towards truth and enlightenment.

You are the destroyer of ignorance, the grantor of knowledge,

And the embodiment of divine grace.

A Call for Divine Intervention

"Oh Divine Presence, hear our humble prayer:

Melt away the karmic bonds that bind us,

And free us from the burdens we carry.
Let your grace flow like a river, washing over our souls,
Cleansing us of our sins and renewing our spirits."

Transcending Sorrows

"In whatever faith men worship me, even so do I render to them." – Sai Satcharitra, Chapter 4
In the depths of our despair, we turn to you, Baba,
For your compassion knows no bounds.
Lift us from the darkness of sorrow,
And fill our hearts with your light.

A Universal Appeal

May your divine light shine upon all beings, Baba,
Regardless of their path or creed. Guide us all towards peace and harmony,
Uniting us in the shared pursuit of truth and love.

Closing Invocation

Oh, Divine Light, source of all creation, Baba,
We bow before you in humble reverence.
Grant us the strength to overcome our challenges,
And the wisdom to walk the path of righteousness.
In your infinite compassion, we find hope.
In your boundless love, we find peace.

Guide us, protect us, and enlighten us,
Now and forevermore.
Glory to Shirdi Sai Baba
"Why fear when I am here?" – Sai Satcharitra,
Chapter 10

Baba, your teachings resonate through time,
Offering solace to the weary and guidance to the lost.
Your words are a balm to the troubled soul,
And your presence a beacon in the darkness.
May we always remember your promise:
"Those who are devoted to me heart and soul will
naturally feel happiness when they hear these stories."
– Sai Satcharitra, Chapter 3
Oh, Sai Baba, the saint of Shirdi,
We offer our prayers at your lotus feet,
Seeking your blessings and your grace,
Today and forevermore.

Divine Invocation: A Prayer to Lord Narasimha

In the depths of spiritual agony, devotees turn to Lord Narasimha with heartfelt pleas. Fear and turmoil grip their souls, seeking refuge and divine protection. Like Prahlada, who found solace in the Lord's embrace amidst adversity, they seek deliverance and peace in the divine presence of Lord Narasimha, whose grace is their ultimate sanctuary.

Divine Manifestation: Ode to Lord Narasimha

O Lord Narasimha, fierce and mighty,
Who appeared from the pillar's core,
With Sri Maha Lakshmi beside thee,
Grace this moment, we implore.

** **

Divine Presence Amidst Turmoil

In the depths of our fear and vulnerability,
We turn to you, O Protector Divine,
For amidst our spiritual turmoil,
Your presence alone brings peace, sublime.

** **

Salvation Through Chanting

Son of the demon-slaying Prahlada,
Born from the lotus navel's grace,
By chanting Hari's name, we seek refuge,
O divine form, reveal your face.

Embrace of Devotion

beloved of the pure-hearted,
Like young Prahlada, drenched in devotion,

Hold us close, dispel our fears,
O Lord Narasimha, from whom salvation flows.

**

Manifestation of Grace

With motherly care, you protected Prahlada,
Turning torment into a tender embrace,
Oh, beloved of the fearless devotees,
Manifest your divine grace.

** **

Safety in Divine Gaze

In your hands lies the promise of safety;
with a glance, all fears vanish without a trace.
Grant us courage and peace,
O Lord Narasimha, in your divine embrace.

Prayer to Lord Ayyappa

Invocation

O Lord Ayyappa, who blends the essence of Shiva and Vishnu,

Embodiment of the soul's divine form,

Bearer of spiritual wisdom,

Radiant with compassion!

** **

Devotional Hymn

Dispeller of worldly illusions,

At your sacred feet, we seek refuge,
Bearer of meditative wisdom,
We surrender to you, O Lord!

Sacred Meditation
In remembrance of your divine presence,
We bow to your blessed feet,
Vanquisher of worldly afflictions,
We seek refuge in you.

Divine Attributes
With the fragrance of cool sandalwood,
Resonating tranquillity,
Sweet nectar-like peace,
In constant remembrance of you.

Spiritual Bliss
In the joyous pulse of life,
In the sacred resonance of the cosmic sound,
In the highest state of spiritual liberation,
We find solace at your divine feet.

** **

Divine Invocation: Prayer to the Cosmic Mother

In reverence and devotion, we gather our hearts to invoke the presence of the Cosmic Mother, whose divine grace envelops all creation. As we offer our prayers with humility and love, may her boundless compassion illuminate our paths, guiding us towards peace, wisdom, and spiritual fulfilment.

** ** **

Invocation to the Cosmic Mother

O Cosmic Mother, an embodiment of infinite compassion and grace,

You are the source of all creation, nurturing all beings
with boundless love.

In your cosmic embrace, we find solace and
strength,

Guiding us through life's challenges with unwavering
protection.

Praise to the Primordial Energy

You are the primordial energy, manifesting in
myriad forms,

From the gentle breeze to the mighty oceans, from
the twinkling stars to the vibrant earth.

Your divine presence pervades every atom of
the universe,

A reminder of your omnipresence, guiding us towards
spiritual awakening.

Prayer for Wisdom and Surrender

Grant us, O Mother, the wisdom to see your divine
hand in every moment,

To surrender our ego at your lotus feet and embrace
humility and gratitude.

Fill our hearts with devotion and reverence, that
we may serve all beings selflessly,

And recognize the unity of all life in your sacred
cosmic dance.

Blessing of Peace and Strength

Bless us with inner peace and strength to navigate
the journey of life with equanimity,

To face adversity with courage, knowing you are
our refuge.

Illuminate our minds with divine knowledge and
understanding,

That we may walk the path of righteousness, spreading
love and harmony.

Final Invocation and Surrender

O Cosmic Mother, shower your blessings upon us,

Awaken our hearts to the beauty of your divine
presence.

May every breath be an offering of devotion to your
sacred essence,

As we merge into your infinite embrace, forever and
evermore.

Prayer to Lord Shiva

Divine Shiva,

The embodiment of bliss invokes your grace and presence to illuminate our path towards inner peace and universal harmony.

Mind:

Grant us clarity of mind to discern truth from illusion, to cultivate thoughts that uplift and inspire. May our minds be a sanctuary of wisdom and compassion, free from fear and confusion.

Body:

Bless our bodies with strength and vitality, nurturing health and well-being. May we tread the path of life with vigour and resilience, honouring our physical vessel as a sacred temple of the soul?

Soul:

Guide our souls towards spiritual awakening and self-realization. Help us recognize our interconnectedness with all beings, fostering empathy and kindness in our hearts. May our journey be one of profound transformation and divine grace.

Harmony:

Instil in us the virtues of harmony and unity, transcending barriers of race, creed, and nationality. Let love and understanding prevail in our interactions, promoting peace and cooperation among all humanity.

Tranquillity:

Grant us inner tranquillity amidst life's challenges, a calm refuge in turbulent times. May your serene presence soothe our hearts and minds, anchoring us in the peace that transcends all understanding.

In the cosmic dance of creation and destruction, may we find solace in your embrace, O Shiva. May we emerge purified and uplifted in body, mind, and soul, embodying the divine light of Shiva. Om Namah Shivaya.

** ** **

Divine Solace: A Prayer to Lord Shiva

O Lord Shiva,
In your boundless grace, I find solace,
Guiding me through life's intricate maze,
Granting me peace, a tranquil space,
Where truth shines bright, falsehood fades away.

Shield me from dark, malevolent powers,
Let your divine light dissolve all fears,
Through life's twists, like a steady flame,
Let love flow freely, drying every tear.

Protect me as vines in harmonious twine,
Let clarity wash away confusion's line,
Free from fear's grip, strong and serene,
With your grace, let burdens be unbound.

Bless me with joy, untouched and clear,
Grant me wisdom to see without fear,

In humble devotion, I embrace your shrine,
With noble thoughts, let my soul align.
Rekindle your light within my heart,
Burn away faults, a divine restart,
Guide my steps with love so pure and true,
Towards peace and wisdom, born anew.

May your cosmic dance weave creations sublime,
In your embrace, I find peace over time,
Let your divine light ever shine bright,
In my soul, a beacon through day and night.

Om Namah Shivaya.

Divine Grace and Compassion: A Journey to the Cosmic Mother

Introduction

It is my crying heart, a vessel of profound emotion, that has converted my agony into prayers. These prayers are directed to the divine presence of Sri Rama, Sri Raghavendra, and Lord Venkateswara. Originally penned in Telugu, I have translated—and rather transcreated—these heartfelt supplications to convey their depth and spiritual essence. May all my prayers reach the Cosmic Mother, the manifestation of supreme cosmic power in various forms.

Rama Shubhanama!

> *"In the presence of the sacred lotus feet of Lord Sri Rama, I find complete compassion and divine consciousness."*

The invocation to Lord Sri Rama begins with a heartfelt salutation to His divine presence. This verse praises Him as the embodiment of supreme compassion and consciousness, acknowledging His qualities of kindness, love, and paternal care. It highlights that truth itself reverberates within Him, making Him the abode of all virtues. Hanuman's heart resonates with the presence of Sri Rama, who is the divine beacon of universal welfare and auspiciousness.

"Oh, Lord Sri Rama, who brings welfare to the universe, please extend your hand to this child with compassion. Are you not the revolutionary force within the heart?"

Offering our prayers at the lotus feet of the benevolent Lord Sri Rama, we recognize His unparalleled grace and the revolutionary spirit He instils within our hearts.

The Compassionate Grace of Sri Raghavendra

In the Abode of Mantralaya

Sri Raghavendra Swami, the beacon of hope and liberation for devotees, resides in the sacred precincts of Mantralaya. Known for his unwavering commitment to dharma and compassion, he is revered as the embodiment of divine grace.

"Oh, Raghavendra, the compassionate one who resides in the sacred Mantralaya! In the realm of Brindavana, you shine with divine radiance, offering solace and liberation to your devotees."

Devotees find solace in the holy presence of Sri Raghavendra, the divine guru who guides them towards spiritual awakening. The heartfelt plea is for Sri Raghavendra to grace them with his compassion, to uplift their spirits and lead them towards the ultimate truth. The connection between the devotee and the divine guru is a bond of love and surrender, where the devotee offers their heart and soul in complete devotion, trusting in the divine figures to lead them on their spiritual journey.

The Divine Presence of Lord Venkateswara

In the Sacred Abode of Tirumala

"In the divine meditation of Lord Venkateswara, the sacred lord of the seven hills, we find unparalleled solace and divine presence."

The sacred hills of Tirumala are illuminated by the divine presence of Lord Venkateswara, who shines with a captivating radiance. He stands as a beacon of compassion, ready to alleviate the sufferings of His devotees.

"Oh, Lord Venkateswara, with the divine symbols of the Sudarshana Chakra and the Shankha, you bless the hearts of your devotees, transforming their sorrows into spiritual offerings."

In the sacred abode, the devotees offer their hearts, filled with devotion and reverence, to the divine feet of Lord Venkateswara. The spiritual journey is marked by a deep connection with the divine, where the devotees seek the Lord's grace to overcome their karmic burdens and attain spiritual enlightenment.

Embracing Divine Grace: A Spiritual Journey Through the Prayer to Mother Sakthi

In the vast tapestry of spiritual devotion, a profound invocation transcends words—a prayer that resonates with the essence of cosmic energy and divine grace. The prayer to Mother Sakthi, presented here in its sacred form, serves as a timeless pathway for seekers to connect with the universal power that governs all existence.

Invocation of Divine Presence

At the heart of this prayer lies a deep reverence for Mother Sakthi, the embodiment of wisdom and cosmic harmony.

She is hailed as the bearer of the sacred Vedas, symbolizing knowledge that transcends time and illuminates the path of spiritual seekers. Through her divine presence, she manifests as the compassionate protector, wielding the sacred trident to dispel negativity and guide souls towards spiritual evolution.

Dispeller of Darkness and Afflictions

As the prayer unfolds, Mother Sakthi is revered as the destroyer of malevolent forces and the dispeller of afflictions. Her omnipotent grace provides solace and courage to those facing challenges, offering a refuge of peace and spiritual rejuvenation. Devotees find strength in their ability to cleanse the mind and heart, paving the way for inner healing and profound spiritual growth.

Embodiment of Universal Energy

Central to the prayer is the recognition of Mother Sakthi as the cosmic life force, permeating every atom and pulsating through the universe. She is invoked through sacred mantras, resonating with the primal energies of 'Om' and 'Shakti Hreem', symbols of creation and manifestation. In her divine form as the Sri Chakra, she weaves the intricate web of existence, guiding souls towards alignment with higher consciousness.

Pathway to Spiritual Enlightenment

Through reciting this prayer, seekers embark on a transformative journey of spiritual awakening. It is a pathway illuminated by divine grace, leading towards the realization of one's true self and ultimate union with the supreme consciousness. Each verse resonates with the aspirant's quest for inner peace, wisdom, and liberation from the cycles of birth and death.

Invocation of Blessings and Guidance

In conclusion, the prayer to Mother Sakthi is more than a mere recitation—it is a sacred communion with the divine presence that transcends all limitations. It expresses profound gratitude and surrender, invoking her blessings to navigate life's challenges with grace and fortitude. May her divine light illuminate our paths, leading us towards spiritual fulfilment and bliss.

Om Shakti Hreem, Sri Chakra Rupini, Bless us with your grace and divine wisdom, O Mother Sakthi, embodying universal energy. Guide us on the path of spiritual evolution, and shower us with your boundless love and protection.

In embracing Mother Sakthi's divine grace, may we find peace, prosperity, and spiritual fulfilment in every step of our journey.

Spiritual Awakening through Divine Compassion

In the Teachings of Epics

The essence of divine grace and compassion is beautifully illustrated in great epics like the Mahabharata and the Ramayana. In the Mahabharata, Lord Krishna's guidance to Arjuna on the battlefield of Kurukshetra exemplifies the divine intervention that leads to spiritual awakening and the triumph of righteousness.

"Whenever there is a decline in righteousness and an increase in unrighteousness, O Arjuna, at that time I manifest Myself on earth." – Bhagavad Gita, Chapter 4, Verse 7

Similarly, in the Ramayana, Lord Rama's unwavering adherence to dharma and His compassionate acts towards His devotees and even His enemies highlight the profound impact of divine grace.

"The highest form of dharma is compassion towards all living beings." – Ramayana

The Path of Surrender and Devotion

The spiritual journey is an ongoing process of surrendering to the divine will and cultivating a heart filled with devotion and compassion. The teachings of the saints and the epics guide us towards a path of righteousness and spiritual awakening. By embracing the divine qualities of compassion, love, and truth, we align ourselves with the higher purpose of life and experience the transformative power of divine grace.

"Surrender unto me alone. By my grace, you will be freed from all sins. Do not grieve." – Bhagavad Gita, Chapter 18, Verse 66

Conclusion

In conclusion, my heartfelt prayers to Sri Rama, Sri Raghavendra, Lord Venkateswara and Goddess Sakthi echo as powerful cries from the depths of my soul. They reflect my profound yearning for their blessings and divine guidance on this spiritual journey. These prayers signify my inner quest, once challenged by the feeling that my soul's power transcended the limitations of my physical form.

Through devotion and surrender to the divine, I have found alignment and peace. This journey has revealed that my soul's true essence finds fulfilment in connection with cosmic power. With each prayer, I seek to break the circle of birth and death, aspiring for ultimate liberation and merger with the Cosmic Self. May all my prayers reach the Cosmic Mother, the supreme manifestation of cosmic energy, whose divine grace continues to illuminate my path and bless me with spiritual growth and transcendence.

The Healing Symphony: Uniting Body, Mind, and Spirit in Medicine

Introduction: The Deeper Connection

In my journey as an educator in the medical field, I've always believed in transcending the mere memorization of facts. Instead, I endeavoured to weave a tapestry that connects the intricate branches of medicine with the profound realms of body, mind, and spirit.

The Paradox of Knowledge: Embracing Ignorance

I often shared with my students the ancient wisdom that "the more you know, the more you realize how much you don't know." This acknowledgment of our ignorance isn't a weakness but the genesis of true knowledge. Students became my teachers in their quest for learning, constantly refreshing my understanding.

The Divergence from Holistic Healing

Despite the interconnectedness inherent in medicine, I observed a gradual dilution of holistic approaches over time. The pursuit of academic excellence shifted towards narrow goals like postgraduate studies and financial aspirations, side-lining the essence of comprehensive healing.

Drawing Inspiration from Unconventional Sources

Though not from the medical profession, Dr. Chalapathi epitomized the integration of body, mind, and spirit through his mastery of homeopathy. His success stories ignited my curiosity to delve into holistic methodologies like META-Health, seeking a deeper understanding of healing beyond conventional boundaries.

Recognizing META-Health as the pinnacle of integrative medicine, I aspired to excel in it, recognizing its capacity to address the interconnectedness of body, mind, and spirit. Homoeopathy, with its array of wonder drugs, became my tool to alleviate various ailments among students, ranging from stress and anxiety to fear of examinations and skin conditions. With the administration of homeopathic medicines, they found profound relief.

However, despite its proven efficacy, homeopathy is often dismissed by many allopathic doctors who fail to acknowledge it as a legitimate branch of medicine. Even some allopathic practitioners discreetly sought relief from Dr. Kumaraih, a prominent homeopath in Anantapur, for their skin and other ailments yet hesitated to embrace its effectiveness fully. False hypocrisies should vanish, replaced by an openness to confess the healing power that lies within alternative modalities.

The Unifying Power of Medicine

Every branch of medicine holds its unique strengths and limitations. Yet, their synergy, including alternative systems like AYUSH, embodies the essence of integrative medicine. Embracing this unity fosters a holistic approach that transcends individual specialties.

The Spiritual Essence of Healing

True healing extends beyond the physical realm, acknowledging the cosmic energy that permeates all existence. When the motive shifts from exploiting suffering to genuine compassion, healing transcends the boundaries of medicine, becoming a sacred duty.

The Pitfalls of Materialistic Medicine

In the pursuit of profit, the essence of healing often gets overshadowed. Over-reliance on lab investigations and treatments neglects the profound simplicity of addressing ailments with basic care and compassion.

Embracing the Placebo Effect

The power of belief in healing, as evidenced by the placebo effect, underscores the importance of holistic approaches. Beyond medications, genuine care and empathetic counselling can often catalyze profound healing transformations.

The Inner Potential: A Call to Spiritual Perception

The true luminaries often remain obscured in a society enamoured with superficial success. Yet, from a spiritual perspective, perceived inefficiencies may hold deeper significance, serving as catalysts for inner growth and enlightenment.

The Personal Journey: From Dormant Ideas to Spiritual Realization

During my house surgency period, I realized that most health problems, once deemed major, could be resolved with basic medication or even a placebo. This revelation prompted me to explore alternative approaches and publish an article on the placebo effect. My initial motivations for joining the medical field, driven by a desire to heal and make a difference, gradually evolved into a deeper quest for spiritual understanding.

Reflecting on Paradoxes and Complexities

In the pursuit of knowledge and success, I often found myself at odds with societal norms and perceptions. While some viewed me as a philosopher, others misunderstood my inner intentions. I knew my inner potential got blocked and realized that my good intentions lacked NATURE's Sanction. Lots of ideas used to gush through my mind, but there was no outlet for my Life Design is different. The 'Cosmic Doctor' is the right one to judge me, for HE knows who I am, what I am, and what I am supposed to carry out, and HE is the one who creates new ideas and makes them trash after a while. If HE wills it, it happens.

Harmony in Healing

As we navigate the intricate pathways of medicine, let us remember the symphony that unites body, mind, and spirit. Beyond the confines of textbooks and diagnoses lies the essence of true healing—a sacred journey that transcends individual pursuits to embrace humanity's collective well-being.

In the pursuit of healing, let us remember that the greatest transformations occur when we harmonize the physical, mental, and spiritual aspects of our being. Let compassion be our guiding light, and let us strive to heal not only the body but also the soul. Embrace the unity of medicine, for in its synergy lies the power to uplift and heal humanity as a whole.

The Power of Soul

In the vast tapestry of existence, the Power of Soul emerges as a force of profound significance. It touches the very essence of life, resonating with the deepest layers of consciousness and the interconnectedness of all things.

Healing Waters of Thought

At the core of this power lies the realization that thoughts influence water, shaping its very structure. This insight unveils the profound connection between consciousness and the physical world, revealing the potential for healing through the alignment of mind and soul.

The Healing Soul

Souls hold within them the transformative energy that can bring healing to individuals and prevent sickness from taking root. As stewards of this power, we become servants not only to humanity but to the entire universe, recognizing the inherent interconnectedness of all souls.

Purposeful Service

The purpose of life, then, becomes clear: to serve. Through service to others, we tap into the intrinsic power of the soul, affirming our commitment to the well-being of humanity and the elevation of consciousness.

Empowering Transformation

Empowerment becomes a sacred duty, a calling to teach healing practices that empower individuals to heal themselves and others. In this way, the Power of the Soul becomes a catalyst for personal and collective transformation, guiding us towards a harmonious existence.

Transcending Boundaries

As we harness the Power of the Soul, we transcend the limitations of the physical realm. This divine energy has the potential to permeate every aspect of life, ushering in an era where the soul reigns supreme and guides us towards healing, rejuvenation, and transformation.

Universal Service

Embedded within the fabric of the universe is the law of universal service, which calls upon us to offer love, forgiveness, peace, and healing unconditionally. By embracing this law, we become vessels for divine grace, extending our service to all souls with gratitude, obedience, loyalty, and devotion.

Divine Frequencies

The frequencies of the soul hold within them the power to heal, prevent sickness, and rejuvenate life. Through divine love, forgiveness, compassion, and light, we unlock the full potential of our souls, becoming instruments of profound healing and transformation.

Soulful Connection

Every human, animal, or elemental soul possesses its unique frequency and power. By recognizing and honouring this interconnected web of souls, we deepen our connection to the divine and each other, fostering a sense of unity and harmony.

The Journey Inward

Ultimately, the Power of Soul leads us on an inward journey toward the depths of our being. Here, we discover the true purpose of life: to serve, heal, and enlighten. In this sacred endeavour, we find inner peace, joy, and a profound sense of fulfilment.

Gratitude and Surrender

As we walk this path, we express gratitude for the blessings bestowed upon us, recognizing that all credit belongs to the divine. With humility and reverence, we surrender to the higher power that guides us, trusting in its infinite wisdom and love.

Soulful Wisdom

In the silence of our souls, we find wisdom beyond measure. Here, we commune with the divine, receiving guidance, protection, and enlightenment. Through the practice of meditation and mindfulness, we open ourselves to the infinite possibilities that lie within.

Unified Consciousness

Humanity finds its true essence in the unified field of consciousness. Here, divisions dissolve, and we recognize our interconnectedness with all beings. We create a peaceful coexistence through acts of kindness, compassion, and love, realizing the inherent unity that binds us together.

Inner Peace

At the heart of the Power of Soul lies inner peace. Through meditation, prayer, and spiritual practice, we cultivate a sense of serenity that transcends external circumstances. In this state of grace, we find balance, healing, and a profound connection to the divine.

The Journey Continues

As we continue this journey of soulful discovery, may we be guided by the light within, trusting in its wisdom and grace. With each step we take, may we walk in harmony with all beings, spreading love, healing, and compassion wherever we go.

In summary, "The Power of Soul" urges us to reflect on the profound connections between all beings. It prompts us to tap into our innate ability to heal, transform, and uplift ourselves and others. By delving into the depths of our souls, we uncover boundless reserves of love, compassion, and wisdom.

Through acts of service, gratitude, and surrender, we align ourselves with the divine energies that permeate the cosmos, transcending limitations to bring healing and harmony. By embracing this journey, we not only discover our true purpose but also contribute to the greater unfolding of universal consciousness.

Let's embark on this soulful quest with open hearts and minds, recognizing that each step brings us closer to realizing our interconnectedness and unlocking the limitless potential of the human spirit. As we do, may we awaken to the transformative power within us and illuminate the world with the brilliance of our souls.

"Journey of the Soul"

In the quiet depths where silence dwells,

Spiritual aspirants find their wells,

Seeking truths beyond the mundane,

In the sacred dance of heart and brain.

Thoughts ripple like water's flow,

Souls journey where mystic winds blow,

Healing whispers in the silent night,
Guiding seekers toward the light.

Sickness fades in the soul's embrace,
As inner peace finds its rightful place,
A servant to humanity's call,
In unity, we rise and fall.

Empowered by a higher plan,
Soulful seekers walk hand in hand,
Transforming darkness into light,
In the sacred dance of day and night.

Love's gentle touch, a soothing balm,
In the realm of spirit, find your calm,
Unified in service, heart, and soul,
Aspiring toward a higher goal.

So let us tread this path with grace,
In every heart, find our sacred space,
For in the journey of the soul,
We find our purpose, we find our whole.

Transcending Apparent to Absolute: The Spiritual Essence of Diwali"

Diwali, a festival celebrated with fervour and joy, holds deeper significance beyond mere social festivities. It symbolizes the triumph of wisdom over ignorance and

righteousness over evil. Narakasura's defeat, commemorated during Diwali, signifies the victory of good over evil, reminding us of the struggle between light and darkness.

Amidst the vibrant celebrations, it's crucial to focus on the profound spiritual essence underpinning Diwali. While the fireworks and lights dazzle the external world, the true essence lies in illuminating our inner selves. Just as the sound of 'Aum' transitions into silence, Diwali should guide us from the apparent to the absolute, from noise to silence, from external jubilation to inner peace.

The real Diwali lies in kindling the inner light of divine love within our hearts. It's about recognizing the silence beyond the sound, the solitude beyond the hilarity. Every spark, every burst of light, should remind us of the light of consciousness within.

Diwali should not only inspire us to illuminate our surroundings but also to actively seek enlightenment within ourselves. It's about igniting the lamp of wisdom, devotion, and spiritual knowledge. Just as fire purifies everything into ash, true prosperity is found in spiritual awakening, symbolized by the sacred vibhuti or udhi.

As Baba beautifully said, "Vairagya (detachment) is the matchstick, Bhakti (devotion) is the oil, Ekagrata (one-pointedness) is the wick, Theosophy is the flame, and Jnana (knowledge) is the light." When every heart is illuminated with such spiritual light, darkness can never overshadow our souls.

Let us celebrate Diwali not just with external lights but with the radiance of inner illumination. Let every heart be lit with the divine light of Sai consciousness, spreading peace and compassion to all. This Diwali, let us transcend the mundane and embrace the absolute, ushering in a new era of spiritual awakening and enlightenment.

Salutations to the festival of lights that illuminates the path to Sai consciousness.

Transcending Boundaries:
A Soul's Silent Journey

Guided by Divine Silence, An Ethereal Departure

Yearning for Anonymity

I want to be anonymous, so why should the world remember me? There is absolute peace and tranquillity when the world does not identify me, for I fall behind this world's expectations, which look quite different.

Lack of Worldly Accomplishments

I have no worldly accomplishments, either professionally or academically. I am not what you see in your mental frame. I am different, which is true, and the Pancha Bhoothas (Earth, Sky, Fire, Water, and Air) are the witnesses to what I speak, which is nothing but Truth.

Sacred Soul

My soul is so sacred and pure and devoid of any prejudice. It is very strong and unable to fit into the body that all of you see. Sometimes, I feel like kicking my body and liberating my soul.

Longing for Freedom

My soul needs freedom, like a flying bird in the vast sky. This body cannot hold my spirit for long, and I have no mission to fulfil with this body. I frequently get the idea of walking through the river and disappearing.

Binding Forces

Amma, Nanna, Hari, Vasantha, and Ganesh are my binders. They are Pancha (Five) Pranas (the vital life force), the energy that exists in my physical body, and they flow and rejuvenate each cell within it.

End of a Chapter

After the sudden disappearance of our parents and Vasantha, who are my very breath, I should not stretch this body further. I feel that it is a selfish act. I made up my mind to leave the world, which is no longer a place of peace for me.

Struggle with Fate

But my brother, Hari, was my binding force, too, and he shared that he had a mission to perform. I see no such mission to be performed with this body I carry, which is becoming a big burden. I told him that I had come to do something for a noble family, but Nature didn't permit it, and the reasons are unknown.

Accepting Limitations

I knew that I could do everything and anything, but Nature tied up my hands, making me helpless and making my life much worse than any beggar. I am so simple, but my simplicity looks to others like complexity.

Misunderstood Existence

I knew how others looked at me, drew interpretations, and underrated my existence. It is a sin to make such false interpretations without knowing the power of my soul. I am languid to truly express myself fully as I feel it is like boasting about my ego, which God never likes.

Burden of Expectations

I know that I became a big burden, for I could do nothing to share the burdens through all these years of cosmic trauma, and I am fed up with such comic dramas.

Unconditional Love

I know only to share my love, and I never expected to be loved by others. Others will not understand 'My Love', which is beyond their comprehension.

Perception versus Essence

What you see in and about me is not the same as who I am. From a spiritual perspective, I transcend the physical form and am interconnected with the divine or universal consciousness.

My physical body and outward appearance represent only a fraction of my true being. What others perceive about me, and even what you perceive about myself, is considered to be influenced by the illusions and distractions of the material world. A true understanding of the self requires looking beyond surface-level attributes and recognizing the deeper spiritual essence within.

Beyond Earthly Boundaries

I don't belong to this district, state, nation, or even Earth. I care for you from the Ether, for none would object or restrict me from doing so.

The Unfathomable Suffering

You perceive the visible anguish within me and swiftly form conclusions, yet the truth lies beyond surface observations. It isn't merely a consequence of lacking worldly achievements or fame. Rather, it pertains to an indescribable realm that defies expression, and even if conveyed, it would remain beyond the grasp of worldly understanding. These depths persist as cosmic mysteries.

A Humble Departure

I need no publicity, and you throw all my literature and books into SAI DHUNI or into flowing waters. There should be no traces of mine in the world.

Transcending Illusions: Finding Unity in Spiritual Awakening

Embracing Spiritual Insights

In the symphony of existence, I am but a note resonating with the essence of love, untainted by the cacophony of competition. My soul finds nourishment when lost in the sacred scriptures of Health, Soul, Spirituality, Mysticism, and the alchemical fusion of Science and Spirituality. Among these sacred tomes, homeopathic texts hold a cherished place, whispering secrets of the soul's journey through the vessel of the body. Books were my best friends, and each selective book is unique.

Divine Revelations in the Mundane

Once, I dreamt of a world bathed in the divine light of integration, where the dance of unity and harmony reigned supreme. Yet, in the tumult of modernity, this vision remains a distant echo, drowned out by the clamour of unhealthy ambition. While the world around me throbs with the pulse of rivalry, I stand apart, a humble pilgrim on the path of enlightenment, untouched by the allure of earthly glory. For in the cosmic dance of existence, I have surrendered to the gentle sway of the divine, free from the burdens of comparison and regret.

Awakening Through Nature's Symphony

Behold the miracles that adorn our sacred tapestry of life: the delicate bloom of jasmine, the bountiful harvest of fruit-laden trees, the sacred alchemy of a cow, transforming humble grass and water into the elixir of life. I used to hug trees and plants and feel oneness with them. They listen and respond, but we lack the sensitive thread to feel it. Every night, I used to observe the vast universe, the sky, the moon, the stars, the planets, and the clouds; oh, I feel that Nature is beautiful and enigmatic. Amidst these wonders, humanity remains ensnared in the illusion of separation, blind to the mystic symphony of Nature's song.

Fragrance of Spiritual Awakening

In these moments of transcendence lies the fragrance of spiritual awakening – a gentle breeze that carries us beyond the confines of the material realm and into the embrace of the divine. It is in this surrender to the rhythm of the cosmos that true fulfilment is found, transcending the ephemeral desires of earthly conquest and awakening to the timeless wisdom of the soul.

Seeking Spiritual Guidance

I like few spiritual discourses, Sadhguru Sri Ravi Shankar Guruji and Sadguru Sri Jaggi Vasudev. See their eyes and gestures, and they look so normal and appear to be speaking to people, but they are connected with the Supreme Master from whom they derive energy. In turn, they radiate among millions of devotees who seek guidance. They have answers for all questions one poses, whether they are a devotee or an atheist. There are solutions to questions from all walks of life, from Spirituality to Science, Optimism to Mysticism, polity to purity, and many more, which people think cannot be answered. All cannot become Masters, and all cannot pretend to be Masters.

The Peace in Being a Follower

There is peace in being a follower rather than assuming the role of a Master, for Masters have the threat from their pseudo disciples who, after a few years, intend to replace their Gurus and set up their kingdom to attract their set of devotees.

Reflections on Present-day Gurus

Here, I quote a few of my experiences. I met a person whose name ends with Baba in the Kurnool District. When I entered, the local priest called me and told me this was not where I should visit. The baba called me by my name, and I was about to go to him, but the priest silently prevented my interaction with him. Through years of SADHANA, one attains SIDHIS, varying from a few to many. Still, they see their end if used indiscriminately to popularize themselves and assign work to senseless senses again. I prefer to remain anonymous, unidentified by the world around me.

To quote another incident, I knew one mimicry artist, and I was told that he became a Guru, propagating the philosophy of SHIRI SAI BABA; out of curiosity, I wanted to meet him. In fact, I met him to find out what triggered him to transform and assume his new role. I could feel that he wanted me to leave the place, and I left with no impression.

One more person, by name ending in Baba, from Kurnool was imitating Bhagwan Sri Sathya Sai Baba, and one day, I sought clarification from Bhagwan Sri Ram Sir, who also sat next to me to see Baba in Puttaparthy. He told me, 'Nagaraj, it is God's Drama, and HE is enjoying it. What's our problem? But remember, Imitation is an Invitation to MAYA".

Power of Silence

Present-day Gurus are involved in quarrelsome debates; of course, it is their choice. But it spreads negative signals in society. It is better to lose a meaningful debate than to fight, exchanging acrimonious words. The great incarnations like Sri Rama Krishna Paramahamsa, Sri Ramana Maharshi, Sri Shiridi Saidev, Bhagwan Sathya Sai, Sri Kanchi Paramacharya, Chandra Sekhar Swamiji, Masters of Ramachandra Mission, Sringeri Jagadguru, Parampara of Mahavatar Babaji, from Lahari Mahasaya to Paramahamsa Yoga Nanda, Bodarshi Calluru Venkata Narayana Swamy, Bhagwan Sriram Sir, many others known to me or unknown to me resort to Silence since their Silence answers our doubts or dilemmas. 'Silence' is beautiful because it does what words cannot convey: communicate, resolve, or appease.

The Heart's Call to Unity

In life, we often feel a tug-of-war between our hearts and minds. It's like they're singing different songs. The mind tends to focus on "I", nurturing our ego and making us feel like the hero. But the heart sings a different tune, one of "we", showering love and reminding us that we're all connected in something bigger than ourselves. God is the real hero; we are zeros when HE is absent in our Lives. God is the ultimate protagonist, the source of all light and love in the grand tapestry of existence. When His presence permeates our lives, we find purpose and meaning, our journey guided by His divine wisdom and grace. Without Him, we are empty vessels devoid of direction and significance, mere zeros in the vast equation of life. Through His presence, our souls are awakened, our paths illuminated, and our hearts filled with the richness of His love.

Our hearts break when we let our minds take over, playing their deceitful games. But when we stay true to our hearts, we feel connected to something greater, something divine. So, let's open our hearts and let in the energy of the universe. Let's remember that we're all in this together and that love is the most powerful force of all. Let's listen to our hearts and let them guide us on our journey.

In the journey of spiritual awakening and connection, amidst the wonders of existence and the trials of modernity, lies the call of the heart. It beckons us to transcend the illusions of separation and ego, embracing the unity of all beings in the divine symphony of life. Through embracing the rhythm of the cosmos and the wisdom inherent in the soul, we discover genuine fulfilment and purpose, transcending the mundane and aligning with the divine flow of existence. Let us heed the whisper of our hearts, for therein lies the profound truth of love and unity, guiding us on our sacred journey of growth and transformation.

The Path of Universal Love: A Journey Towards Spiritual Enlightenment

Universal Love is the foundation of any religion, yet it seems conspicuously absent today. Religion, originally intended as a bridge between God and devotees, has unfortunately become an obstacle.

There is no competition among Gods because they are all one. Each incarnates from Heaven in different forms, such as Shiva, Buddha, Jesus, Rama, Krishna, and many other Goddesses. God is simple; everything else is complex, and we made it. As we become more modern, reaching the Moon and Space, unhealthy competition arises between narrow-minded individuals following different faiths and cults, causing societal splits, conflicts, and unrest. A truly spiritual person adores oneness and inclusiveness and realizes the truth behind different incarnations.

In the realm of divinity, there's no competition among the Gods, as they're all part of the same divine essence. Each comes from a singular heavenly source. This divine simplicity contrasts with the complexity we humans have built around it.

This insight calls us to transcend the divisive boundaries of religious identities and embrace the essence of unity that underlies all faiths. By recognizing the divine presence in all beings and honouring the various manifestations of the divine, we can foster harmony, understanding, and peace in our communities and the world at large.

Let us strive to embody the spirit of universal love and inclusivity as we navigate the complexities of religious diversity, knowing that in unity lies our strength and our salvation.

Spirituality takes flight when the boundaries of religion fade away. The search for God must now turn inward into the depths of the human heart. True spirituality often flourishes when the constraints of organized religion are left behind.

For those who identify as 'spiritual' rather than 'religious,' embodying personified purity, unshaken character, simplicity, divinity, universal love, and humility is essential. This requires consistent and unwavering penance, heart purification, and liberation from the illusions of the egoic mind. One can transcend only through communion with the divine, both within and outside.

Unlimited spiritual or supernatural powers, referred to as "Siddhis," are attainable by shedding the egoic "I" and being attuned to the cosmic 'eye'. However, these powers must be wielded with humility and selflessness, as they can otherwise lead one astray into a realm devoid of basic virtues.

The Yogi who achieves the highest stage of salvation, self-actualization, or realization will find themselves in harmonious accord with nature. Salvation entails complete liberation from all sensory temptations and pleasures. 'Devotion' is vital in pursuing the ultimate goal: seeing God in oneself and others, including all creatures transcending all dualities.

Meditation does not induce a loss of consciousness; it entails maintaining conscious awareness while distancing oneself from Maya's illusory web. Liberation from attachment, the illusion of ownership, and egoic identification as the doer of actions are all essential steps toward spiritual awakening.

The mere contemplation of purity, the very essence of purity, bestows immense bliss and showering grace. The soul, inherently pure and unalloyed, may be temporarily obscured by the shadow of the mayic mind. However, through heightened awareness, one can transcend the limitations of the ego and embrace true wisdom (gnana), fearlessness, mental stability, and self-respect.

It's crucial to recognize that the Astral Body can only emit vibrations when the individual's Budhi, or intellect, is pure to the core. Therefore, empowerment comes through the purity of the soul.

Let us remember that the journey towards spiritual enlightenment is not merely a personal endeavour but a collective awakening of humanity. May we walk this path with humility, compassion, and unwavering dedication, guided by the light of universal love and the wisdom of unity, knowing that each step brings us closer to the divine essence within and outside? Let the Purity of the Soul empower us all and help us reach a world wherein peace and harmony reign supreme.

Unveiling Mysteries: Insights into Miracles and Cosmic Energy

Paramhansa Yogananda's teachings transcend conventional wisdom, exploring miracles as profound expressions of cosmic energy and divine intervention. These insights provoke deeper spiritual contemplation by challenging ordinary perceptions of existence.

Miracles: Beyond Physical Laws

According to Yogananda, miracles are not anomalies but manifestations of divine will operating beyond physical laws. For instance, Mahavatar Babaji's reputed ability to materialize and dematerialize his physical form illustrates mastery over cosmic energies. Similarly, Christ's resurrection exemplifies divine intervention transcending human comprehension.

Science and Maya: Limits of Understanding

While science provides valuable insights into the physical universe governed by Maya, the cosmic illusion, Yogananda suggests that true enlightenment surpasses intellectual analysis. For example, Newtonian mechanics and Einstein's theories offer frameworks within Maya's realm, yet spiritual realization unveils a deeper unity underlying all creation.

The Role of Light and Energy

Einstein's theory of relativity, especially the constant velocity of light, serves as a foundational principle in understanding cosmic energy. Yogananda often likens this energy to creative cosmic light rays through which miracles unfold. This perspective underscores how spiritual masters harness these cosmic energies beyond conventional physical laws.

Spiritual Mastery and Divine Will

Central to Yogananda's teachings is spiritual mastery, where individuals transcend material consciousness and temporal constraints. For example, Lahiri Mahasaya's ability to commune with higher realms and manifest healing energies demonstrates alignment with divine will, showcasing the transformative power of spiritual realization.

The Quest for Unity and Enlightenment

Yogananda emphasizes that humanity's ultimate goal is to transcend duality and perceive the unity of the creator. This journey involves practices like meditation and self-realization, which dissolve the illusions of Maya. By embracing spiritual insights, individuals can achieve liberation and a deeper understanding of their cosmic purpose.

The Power of Cosmic Energy

Cosmic energy, as elucidated by Paramhansa Yogananda, is the fundamental force underlying all existence. It transcends the limitations of physical laws, operating at the level of consciousness and divine will. This energy is the creative essence that sustains the universe and manifests miracles. For instance, spiritual masters harness cosmic energy to perform extraordinary feats like instantaneous healing or materialization. Yogananda teaches that by attuning oneself to this cosmic energy through meditation and spiritual practices, individuals can experience profound life transformations. This cosmic energy not only facilitates physical and spiritual healing but also nurtures a deeper connection with the divine, enabling individuals to align with their highest potential and purpose in the cosmic order.

Jesus Christ: The Embodiment of Divine Love

The Meaning of Jesus and Christ

In Hebrew, the name Jesus means "Anointment" or "Consecration," while Christ signifies "Saviour." As we celebrate Christmas, we wish the global Saviour many happy returns of the day. But when we reflect on the essence of Jesus Christ, we realize He transcends the confines of earthly dates. Christ lived before the first Christmas and continues to live beyond Good Friday. He is the source and force of life itself, an elixir by His very being and the omnipresent cosmic consciousness.

The Contrast Between Worldly Unrest and Divine Bliss

While the world grapples with unrest and discontent, Christ remains ever-happy, embodying bliss and divine joy. The world's turmoil stems from turning away from the voice of the Lord and unthinkingly following Satan's path. To restore harmony, we must abandon these misguided ways and embrace Christ's footsteps, drinking deeply from the nectar of His bliss.

Embodying Sacrifice, Love, and Compassion

Christ represents a crystallized and concretized form of sacrifice, love, compassion, peace, and light. His sacrifice was driven by compassion for humanity, and His incarnation was to save a forlorn world. The essence of religion, derived from the Latin "religare," means "to tie back." Religion should bind us together, encouraging us to strive as one to reach the divine.

Unity of Religions and the Pursuit of God

All religions are like sacred rivers, each flowing toward the same vast ocean. The aim of every river is to reach the sea, just as the goal of every religion is to reach God. In the sacred river of Christianity, a true Christian is like a pure water drop reflecting Christ's love. This metaphor beautifully illustrates the unity of all spiritual paths, each contributing to the divine journey.

Discovering the Sacred Within

To truly connect with Jesus Christ, we must search for a church deep within our hearts. It is there, within the sanctuary of our soul, that we discover His presence. The sacred spirit of Jesus acts as a guiding torch, illuminating our path and encouraging us to march ahead. With His divine light, we can journey towards godhood, embodying His teachings of love and compassion.

Embracing the Teachings of Jesus

The teachings of Jesus Christ are a beacon of hope and love in a world often overshadowed by darkness. His message transcends religious boundaries, offering a universal call to love, compassion, and unity. By following His example, we can transform our lives and the world around us, creating a more harmonious and compassionate global community.

In this spiritual journey, let us embrace the sacred essence of Jesus Christ, allowing His love to guide us. By embodying His teachings, we can find peace within ourselves and extend it to the world, reflecting His divine light and love in every action.

Infinite Connections: Tales of Divine Encounters

In the tapestry of existence, each encounter with the divine serves as a beacon of light, guiding us along the path of spiritual awakening. Through moments of grace and moments of mystery, we are reminded of the presence that resides within and around us, illuminating our journey with the radiance of divine love. May we tread the path with humility and devotion, ever attuned to the whispers of the divine sparks that ignite our souls?

Soulful Encounters

In the hallowed halls of spiritual discourse, I found myself enraptured by the teachings of Gurudev Sri Ganapathi Sachidananda Swamy in Hyderabad. Seeking the sacred touch of Their divine feet, I was met with Their profound response: "What was to be given has already been bestowed upon you." Puzzled, I retreated into the depths of silence, recognizing the abundance of the divine presence within.

Later, as I immersed myself in prayer, Swamy graced me with a radiant smile, blessing me with divine favour. Inspired by Their presence, I composed hymns and poetry, offerings of devotion that circulated among our circle, each word resonating with the essence of divine grace.

Embracing the Divine Essence

In the embrace of Mother Vijayeswaridevi, known as Karunamayi Amma, whose incarnation was foretold by the revered Bhagwan Ramana Maharshi, I was enveloped in the warmth of love. Her tender gaze bestowed upon me the title of "Raja," and in moments of divine communion, saffron blessings flowed from their sacred toes, materializing into the form of Lord Vinayaka. Mother asked me to run the Hospital that intends to start in Bangalore. It did not materialize, and I believe that for each of your wishes, the grace of the cosmic mother should prevail.

In the tapestry of spirituality, there often emerge figures who seem to impede our connection with the divine, acting as barriers to our moments of transcendence.

However, within this intricate dance of existence, they, too, play a part, perhaps as instruments of divine play, challenging us to delve deeper into the mysteries of our spiritual journey. Their presence prompts us to confront obstacles and seek understanding, revealing hidden layers of meaning and significance. In navigating these encounters, we may uncover profound insights into the nature of existence and our relationship with the divine. Thus, even amidst the challenges they present, there lies a subtle invitation to explore the profound depths of spiritual wisdom and growth.

With each encounter, I was reminded of the unpredictable yet undeniable presence of the divine in our lives. Though beyond comprehension, these manifestations served as poignant reminders of the boundless love that permeates all existence.

Pilgrimages of Spiritual Awakening

Fuelled by a deep spiritual longing, I embarked on pilgrimages to holy shrines, guided by the invisible hand of destiny. In the sanctified presence of Guru Raghavendra Swamy in Mantralayam, I found solace and devotion. Through acts of love and devotion, such as composing the Sri Raghavendra Swamy Stotram, I sought to express my reverence and gratitude.

On a particular date, which might be in 2018, my brother and I were there near Brundavanam. It was closing time, and there was another person, but the security guard asked us to finish Dharshan quickly as it was almost 1.50 in the afternoon, and the temple authorities were about to close the main door. My brother first noticed a small bronze idol of Shirdi Sai wearing KAFNI cloth, and he just asked me to see the idol before Raghavendra Swamy Brundavanam, and I told him that it was the idol of Sai of Shirdi. Both were dumbfounded and shocked for a while, and we left the holy shrine with a nostalgic feeling.

In moments of divine convergence, as we stood amidst Raghavendra Swamy's sanctum, the boundaries of time and space seemed to dissolve, unveiling Shirdi Sai's sacred presence. It was as if the two divine energies converged, merging into one harmonious essence that permeated the air around us.

With awe in our hearts, we witnessed miracles unfold before our very eyes, each moment a testament to the ineffable mysteries of divine grace. The air was pregnant with a sense of wonder and reverence as we beheld the divine manifestations, and we felt humbled by the sheer magnitude of the divine presence.

In this sacred space, where the realms of the seen and unseen intertwined, we were reminded of the interconnectedness of all things and the omnipresence of the divine. It was a profound experience that left an indelible mark on our souls, igniting a flame of devotion that burned brightly within us.

As we departed from that holy shrine, we carried with us memories of the miracles witnessed and a renewed sense of faith and purpose. For in those moments of divine convergence, we were reminded that the divine is ever-present, guiding and protecting us on our journey through life.

Fuelled by a deep spiritual longing, I embarked on pilgrimages to holy shrines, guided by the invisible hand of destiny. In the sanctified presence of Guru Raghavendra Swamy in Mantralayam, I found solace and devotion. Through acts of love and devotion, such as composing the Sri Raghavendra Swamy Stotram, I sought to express my reverence and gratitude.

In my frequent visits to places like Kasapuram, Nemakallu, and Muridi, I am drawn irresistibly to the idol of Lord Hanuman. His eyes, reflecting the essence of Vayu, the wind god, hold a mesmerizing allure. Despite my brother's reminders of the passing of time, I find myself yearning to linger until the temple doors close for the night. With a heavy heart, I eventually tear myself away, feeling a deep reluctance to depart from the divine presence.

I am completely absorbed in those sacred moments, oblivious to the world around me. The sight of Lord Hanuman fills me with a sense of connection and belonging, as if I am standing in his divine presence and sharing my joys and sorrows with him. It is as though he understands my every emotion, offering solace and companionship in moments of both agony and ecstasy.

The Divine Feast: Nourishment for My Hungry Soul

Yearning for Spiritual Fulfilment

In my quest for spiritual fulfilment, I often yearn for a deeper connection, a sense of divine presence that satiates my inner hunger and quenches my spiritual thirst. This longing for spiritual sustenance is a common thread that weaves through the fabric of all faiths and belief systems, emphasising our universal need for divine grace.

A Personal Invocation

The journey begins with a heartfelt invocation, "O! My Lord of the Inner Heart!" This opening line signifies an intimate and personal relationship with the divine, setting the stage for a profound spiritual exploration. The divine thoughts are depicted as a "festive feast" to my hungry soul, illustrating the richness and abundance found in spiritual communion.

Thirst and Hunger for the Divine

As the spiritual journey progresses, the imagery of thirst and hunger intensifies. My heart and throat feel parched, symbolizing the deep longing for divine mercy. This yearning is met with the boundless mercy of the divine, described as "pacific" and "vast." The stark contrast between my human need and divine abundance highlights the transformative power of divine grace.

The Dual Nature of Existence

Exploring the dual nature of existence—the physical and the spiritual—is crucial. The line "My psyche and soul do belch and burst, deprived of Thy food and fruit" reflects the inner turmoil and emptiness that arise from spiritual deprivation. Yet, my plea for grace signifies hope and the possibility of renewal through divine intervention.

Attributes of the Divine

The poem further delves into the attributes of the divine, portraying the divine as the "Cosmic Flood of Light" and the "Supreme Source of Might." These portrayals emphasize the omnipotence and omnipresence of the divine, whose forgiveness and salvation are central to my faith. Sacred scriptures are depicted as the breath of life, and divine words as the manna of hope, illustrating the vital role of holy texts and divine guidance in nurturing my soul.

Confronting Evil

Acknowledging the presence of evil in the world, the poem represents it as a force that has "stolen my daily bread." This metaphor extends to the broader context of a world haunted by darkness and devoid of true dawn. Despite this, there is a rallying cry for the sacred spirit to awaken, a powerful call for divine intervention to restore balance and bring forth light.

Embracing Divine Grace

In essence, "The Divine Feast" is a profound reflection on my human condition, my insatiable hunger for divine connection, and the transformative power of spiritual nourishment. It serves as a reminder of the ever-present grace available to me and the enduring hope for a world illuminated by divine light.

Universal Spiritual Journey

This spiritual article, inspired by the poem, invites me to contemplate my own spiritual journey and recognize the boundless grace that awaits in the divine feast. By connecting with the divine across all faiths, I find the nourishment my soul seeks, transcending religious boundaries to embrace the universal truth of divine love and mercy.

In this journey, I am reminded that the divine presence is a constant source of light and strength, guiding me through the darkest of times. The sacred texts, the words of wisdom, and the infinite mercy of the divine all serve to sustain my spirit and nurture my soul. This universal truth resonates across all spiritual paths, offering hope and solace to every seeker of the divine feast.

The Divine Feast

O! My Lord of the Inner Heart!

Thy thought is a festive feast.

To the hungry soul on fast . . .

Thirsty are my heart and throat Alike pacific,

Thy mercy is so vast . . .

My psyche and soul do belch and burst,

Deprived of Thy food and fruit . . .

Grace me, Father, Jesus Christ!

Thou art Godhood

And Doyen of Sainthood . . .

Thou art the Cosmic Flood of Light and the Supreme
Source of Might...

Forgiveness is Thy blood

And Thou art the Saviour of the world . . .

The Holy Bible is my breath.

The manna of hope is Thy word.

Reanimated brutal Satan

Animated his evil and dead . . .

And has stolen our daily bread . . .

Earth has haunted nights with no true dawn . . .

The devilish world is now at stake!

Sacred spirit of 'Christ,' awake!!

Embracing the Sacred Journey of Emotions: A Spiritual Perspective

Life's emotional spectrum is a divine tapestry intricately woven with feelings that guide our spiritual evolution. Each emotion serves as a sacred messenger, inviting us to deepen our connection with the divine and our inner selves. By recognizing and embracing the spiritual essence of our emotions, we transform our inner landscape and align ourselves with divine wisdom.

The Subtle Guidance of Anger and Apathy

"In the Bhagavad Gita, Lord Krishna teaches, 'Anger leads to clouding of judgment, which results in bewilderment of the memory. When memory is bewildered, intelligence is lost, and when intelligence is lost, one falls back into the material world.'" - Bhagavad Gita 2:63

At the dawn of our spiritual journey, we encounter gentle nudges in the form of mild irritation and apathy. These emotions are sacred signals urging us to turn inward and cultivate serenity. By responding with patience and compassion, we honour these divine invitations and move towards a higher state of spiritual awareness.

As we advance on our path, we may face more intense emotions such as resentment and hostility. These profound feelings challenge us to transcend ego-driven reactions and embrace forgiveness and understanding. By transforming anger and deep-seated hostility into acts of humility and empathy, we elevate our spiritual vibration and align with the divine harmony. Engaging in meditation and self-reflection helps us transmute these energies into profound love and spiritual strength.

Transforming Shame and Guilt into Divine Lessons

Shame and guilt are powerful forces that shape our spiritual journey, revealing both our human vulnerabilities and our potential for divine transformation.

Feelings of self-consciousness and awkwardness invite us to embrace our authentic selves with grace. When we confront embarrassment and regret, we are called to practice self-acceptance and trust in divine guidance. By integrating these experiences, we purify our souls and align ourselves with the divine will.

When faced with intense feelings of humiliation or self-condemnation, we have an opportunity for profound spiritual awakening. These challenging emotions invite us to rise above our suffering, seek divine forgiveness, and transform our inner turmoil into wisdom through deep introspection and spiritual practice.

Navigating Fear, Anxiety, and Panic as Spiritual Catalysts

Fear and anxiety are natural aspects of the human experience but also serve as catalysts for spiritual growth.

Feelings of apprehension and caution remind us to trust in the divine plan. By surrendering our fears through prayer and meditation, we embrace the unknown with faith and confidence. These gentle emotions guide us toward spiritual surrender and divine trust.

Intense feelings of panic and terror challenge us to anchor ourselves in the divine presence. Through deep spiritual practice and surrender, we transcend these overwhelming emotions and discover peace amidst the chaos of life.

Transforming Jealousy and Envy into Spiritual Wisdom

Jealousy and envy often arise from a sense of lack and comparison but offer pathways to spiritual fulfilment.

Feelings of insecurity and suspicion prompt us to focus on our unique spiritual journey. By cultivating gratitude and letting go of attachments, we align ourselves with divine abundance and spiritual contentment.

Intense emotions of greed and resentment can be consuming but also hold the potential for spiritual liberation. By detaching from material pursuits and seeking spiritual nourishment, we transform these emotions into inner peace and a deeper connection with the divine.

Celebrating Happiness, Contentment, and Joy as Divine Gifts

Positive emotions such as happiness, contentment, and joy are divine gifts that enrich our spiritual journey.

Feelings of amusement and peacefulness remind us to cherish the present moment and reflect our alignment with the divine. By celebrating life's blessings and nurturing these emotions, we cultivate lasting inner peace and joy.

Intense states of ecstasy and bliss are moments of divine communion. Through dedicated spiritual practice, we sustain these elevated states and connect with the infinite source of divine love, experiencing a profound sense of unity with the divine presence.

Transcending Sadness, Grief, and Depression

Sadness and grief are natural responses to loss, while depression is a more persistent state. These emotions offer pathways to spiritual growth.

Feelings of disappointment and melancholy invite us to reflect deeply on our experiences and seek divine healing. By embracing our humanity and turning to spiritual guidance, we transform these emotions into resilience and strength.

Intense despair and hopelessness hold the potential for profound spiritual transformation. By surrendering our suffering to the divine and seeking higher wisdom, we find peace through deep spiritual practice and connection with the divine embrace.

The journey of life is a sacred dance with our emotions, each one offering a unique opportunity for spiritual growth and transformation. By understanding and embracing our emotions with compassion and awareness, we can navigate the complex landscape of our inner world and align ourselves with the divine. Through this journey, we discover that every emotion, whether soft or intense, is a step closer to our true spiritual essence.

Moving Forward by Looking Inward: An Indicator of Ripened Wisdom

In our profound dialogue with Sri Sri Sri Vidyanarayana Theertha of Badrika Mutt, my brother, Dr. Hari, and I engaged in an enlightening exploration of genuine progress. This conversation illuminated the understanding that true advancement is not merely about external accomplishments but is deeply rooted in inner reflection and spiritual awakening. Swamy emphasized the necessity of transcending superficial desires and connecting with our inner spiritual essence. His guidance encourages us to look beyond the fleeting material realm and align with the divine core of our being. This article integrates timeless wisdom from epics and scriptures to provide insights on achieving inner peace, overcoming material cravings, and embracing a profound divine companionship. It offers a path to deeper self-realization and spiritual fulfilment, reflecting the essence of our transformative dialogue.

Reflecting on the Past

The past is immutable and cannot be changed. However, it provides essential lessons that inform our present actions. This reflection should not be clouded by regret but should focus on the insights gained. For instance, Arjuna's contemplation on the battlefield in the Bhagavad Gita led him to profound realizations about his purpose and actions, demonstrating how reflection can guide us toward spiritual clarity and fulfilment.

Awakening Awareness

Without true awareness, one may accumulate knowledge yet remain spiritually ignorant. This is akin to the tale of Ravana from the Ramayana. Despite his immense knowledge and power, Ravana's ignorance of true wisdom led to his downfall. This illustrates the importance of integrating spiritual awareness with knowledge for genuine self-realization and transformation.

Inner Peace vs. External Cravings

The search for external peace often results in temporary satisfaction, akin to a sugar-coated pill. The Bhagavad Gita teaches that true peace arises from 'Inner Purity' and 'Innate Sanctity'. Dhruva's story from the Vishnu Purana is a powerful example. His unwavering devotion and inner purity led to spiritual fulfilment and divine blessings, showing that lasting peace comes from within rather than from external achievements.

Mastering the Mind

The mind's dominance can detract from our spiritual essence. Sensory stimulation and fleeting pleasures often lead us astray. The sage Narada's experiences in the Puranas highlight the importance of mastering the senses and focusing on the divine rather than being ensnared by sensory illusions and distractions.

Recognizing the Power of Illusion

The mind's illusions can create a false sense of uniqueness and separation. This power of illusion often blinds us to the divine assistance that supports us. King Yudhishthira's trials in the Mahabharata teach us about the nature of illusion and the divine presence that helps us navigate through challenges, reminding us that we are not alone in our spiritual journey.

Connecting with the Inner Conscience

True progress involves aligning with the soul and inner conscience rather than seeking external validation. King Harishchandra's sacrifice in the name of truth illustrates how aligning with inner values and spiritual purpose leads to true advancement and divine favour.

Re-Evaluating Success and Failure

Success and failure, as defined by worldly standards, are transient. True success is found in experiencing the divine presence and unconditional love. Prahlada's unwavering devotion to the Bhagavata Purana, despite facing severe trials, exemplifies how true success is measured by spiritual triumph and divine grace rather than material achievements.

Embracing Divine Companionship

Rather than seeking to fully understand the divine, it is more profound to accept it as an eternal companion. Prayer for experiential wisdom helps dissolve barriers and move closer to God's everlasting peace. The story of Sudama in the Bhagavata Purana, whose simple devotion and humility were met with divine grace, underscores the importance of a sincere, heartfelt connection with the divine.

Maintaining Stillness Amidst Storms

The power of illusion originates in the mind, certifying the authenticity of all deeds. It often makes one feel unique and distinct from the rest of the world, deluding them into believing they are the doer of all actions, forgetting the "Invisible Helping Hands" that protect them from illusion's grasp. Allow your inner conscience to check your running mind. Moving forward is not about social status, economic security, or knowledge accumulation but about establishing a link with your soul.

True Success and the Divine Presence

Do not let changing fortunes perturb you. Reflect on what failure, success, misery, and happiness truly mean. The real failure is the inability to feel and experience the divine presence. True success is not in earning riches or praise but in experiencing the warmth of divine love. This transient world's success is fleeting, like water bubbles or moving clouds. Real success lies in experiencing the divine presence.

Let us strive to move forward by looking inward, guided by divine grace. By reflecting on our inner selves and embracing the lessons of the past, we can progress meaningfully. Aligning our actions with our inner wisdom and spiritual essence allows us to experience the transformative power of divine love and achieve true, lasting peace. Through introspection and spiritual alignment, we uncover a deeper understanding of the divine and our place within the cosmic order.

Divine Dialogues: Dr Hari's Enlightening Conversation with Sri Sri Sri Vidyanarayana Theertha

This enlightening conversation between Dr Hari and Sri Sri Sri Vidyanarayana Theertha of Dwaraka Peetam explores the profound concept of inner energy and the influence of Maya—the illusion that keeps us in ignorance. Swamy emphasizes the importance of self-inquiry, recognizing the divine in every aspect of creation, and the role of the SADGURU in guiding us toward spiritual realization.

Through parables and quotes from the Bhagavad Gita and Upanishads, Swamy illustrates the path to inner peace, the necessity of unwavering faith in the Master, and the transformation that occurs through devotion and surrender. This conversation serves as a timeless guide for those seeking spiritual enlightenment and the bliss of divine grace.

Swamy, originally a doctor by profession, renounced his earthly life at a young age to become a sanyasi and later a mystic monk. He has a special liking for our family and has visited us a couple of times. My brother has been frequently called upon by Swamy, and their association is believed to date back to previous lives. I found their discussion profoundly enlightening and felt compelled to share it here. May all who read this in the future experience the bliss of their spiritual exchange. He is the one who wrote about me,' You get MD, but mentioned it is Master of Divinity"

** ** **

Dr. Hari: *Swamy, our very existence is based upon "Inner Energy." Can you explain this supreme energy, which is available in abundance both within us and outside?*

Swamy: Certainly, Dr. Hari. This energy is indeed abundant, but many fail to notice it due to the power of Maya—the illusion that keeps us in complete darkness of ignorance. Think of Maya as a dense fog that obscures the sunlight. The sunlight is always there, but the fog prevents us from seeing it clearly.

As described in the Bhagavad Gita, "Maya is Mine, made of the gunas; difficult it is to pierce. Those who come to Me, they cross over this Maya" (Bhagavad Gita 7.14).

Consider this parable: A man once lived in a house with closed windows and doors, never realizing the bright, beautiful world outside. Only when he opened a window did he see the light and vibrant colours of the world. Maya is like that closed house, keeping us in darkness until we open the window of inner awareness.

Dr. Hari: Why do we get entangled in the web of temporal joys and end up with abysmal memories?

Swamy: Our entanglements with the worldly world lead us to temporary joys, much like a fly attracted to a flame. These temporary joys eventually sap our stored energies, leaving us depressed.

"The pleasures that arise from contact are indeed the wombs of pain; they have a beginning and an end, and the wise do not rejoice in them" (Bhagavad Gita 5.22).

Here's a parable: There was once a thirsty crow who found a pot with a little water at the bottom. It dropped pebbles into the pot to raise the water level and quench its thirst. Our pursuit of worldly pleasures is like the crow's effort— temporary satisfaction that requires constant effort, leaving us exhausted in the end.

Dr. Hari: How can we truly celebrate life in its totality?

Swamy: By withdrawing from the mundane world even for a split second and posing deep questions to ourselves, such as "Who am I?" and "What is the purpose of my existence?" It's like taking a moment to step back and see the entire forest rather than getting lost in the trees. As the Upanishads advise, "Tat Tvam Asi" – You are that supreme consciousness.

"As a man thinketh, so he becomes" (Chandogya Upanishad 3.14.1).

Consider the parable of the lion cub raised by sheep. The cub believed it was a sheep until one day it saw its reflection in a pond and heard the roar of a lion. Realizing its true nature, it joined the lions. Similarly, we must realize our true divine nature.

Dr. Hari: What should we appreciate about the Creator's wonderful creation?

Swamy: We should appreciate the vibrant presence in every cell of our body, in the smiles or cries of a baby, the shining Sun, glowing moonlight, blossoming jasmine flowers, speaking parrots, sweet singing cuckoos, running streams, steep mountains, plants bearing fruits, and sprouting seeds. It's like marvelling at a grand symphony where every instrument plays a part in creating harmony.

"The wise see the same in a learned and gentle Brahmin, a cow, an elephant, a dog, and a dog-eater" (Bhagavad Gita 5.18).

There's a parable about a man who found a beautiful garden. Initially, he was only interested in picking the flowers. But as he spent more time there, he began to appreciate the entire garden—the trees, the birds, the streams. He realized the beauty was in the whole garden, not just in the individual flowers.

Dr. Hari: How can we taste the sweetness of His grace?

Swamy: By dropping into the ocean of His bounteous Love and becoming one with Him through unconditional love and unquestionable faith in His Wisdom.

"He who has no attachments can truly love others, for his love is pure and divine" (Bhagavad Gita 3.25).

Here's a parable: A salt doll went to measure the depth of the ocean. As it entered the water, it dissolved, becoming one with the ocean. The doll's quest ended only when it surrendered itself completely to the ocean. Similarly, we must dissolve our ego and merge with the divine to experience His grace.

Dr. Hari: How can we drive away negative energies?

Swamy: Make an effort to maintain positive thinking. Explore yourself to find inner peace and serene mental tranquillity. It's like cleaning a mirror to see your true reflection.

"When a man is free from all desires and is content with the Self alone, he is said to be established in wisdom" (Bhagavad Gita 2.55).

Consider this parable: A king had a diamond covered in dirt. He gave it to a jeweller who carefully cleaned it, revealing its brilliance. Our minds are like that diamond—cleaning away the negativity reveals our true, radiant nature.

Dr. Hari: What is required to evolve beyond the "Little Self"?

Swamy: An inner vision to discover the glory of Divine Cosmic Inner Energy, which burns vices and keeps virtues glowing. Imagine a lamp that dispels darkness; this inner vision is that lamp.

"When a man sees all beings as equal in suffering and in joy, he has attained the highest state of spiritual union" (Bhagavad Gita 6.32).

There's a parable about a sculptor who chisels away at a block of marble to reveal a beautiful statue hidden within. Our inner vision helps us chisel away at our vices, revealing the divine self within.

Dr. Hari: Can we achieve this without the help of SADGURU, the Supreme Master?

Swamy: No, it is impossible to move forward without His grace and guidance. Our efforts are meaningful only with His divine intervention.

"The Guru is the representative of Brahma, Vishnu, and Shiva. He creates, sustains knowledge, and destroys the weeds of ignorance" (Guru Gita).

Think of this parable: A traveller lost in a dense forest found a guide who led him safely to his destination. The guide's knowledge and experience were crucial. Similarly, the SADGURU guides us through the forest of life.

Dr. Hari: What should we do to remember the SADGURU?

Swamy: Engage in Sadhana (Effort) dispassionately, always remembering that the SADGURU is the architect of our life. It's like a sculptor chiselling away at a stone to reveal a beautiful statue within.

"Even the most sinful, if he worships Me with undivided heart, must be accounted righteous, for he has rightly resolved" (Bhagavad Gita 9.30).

There's a parable about a farmer who patiently tends to his crops every day, knowing that the harvest will come in due time. Our Sadhana is like that daily effort, with the SADGURU's guidance leading to spiritual harvest.

Dr. Hari: How should we perceive pain and contentment?

Swamy: See the hidden gain in every pain and be content with whatever you have without regretting unfulfilled aspirations. Remember, "Sarvam Khalvidam Brahma"—everything is indeed Brahman. Even pain has a purpose in our spiritual journey.

"Pleasure and pain, gain and loss, victory and defeat— treat these impostors the same" (Bhagavad Gita 2.38).

Consider this parable: A potter moulds clay into a beautiful pot by applying pressure. The clay undergoes pain, but the end result is a beautiful, useful pot. Similarly, our pains shape us into better beings.

Dr. Hari: What is the role of the GURU in our lives?

Swamy: The GURU is our well-wisher, playing the role of both parent and guide, ensuring our self-realization through His dictum. The GURU's guidance is like a lighthouse for a ship navigating stormy seas.

"One should approach a Guru who is well-versed in the scriptures, who has direct realization of the Truth, and who is calm and self-controlled" (Mundaka Upanishad 1.2.12).

There's a parable about a bird with a broken wing. A kind man nursed it back to health and taught it to fly again. The GURU is like that kind man, helping us heal and soar to our spiritual heights.

Dr. Hari: How can we avoid the influence of MAYA, the Illusion?

Swamy: Be watchful and remember the Master with every heartbeat, avoiding its dangerous influence. It's like keeping a lantern lit in the darkness to avoid stumbling.

"For one who has conquered the mind, the mind is the best of friends; but for one who has failed to do so, his mind will remain the greatest enemy" (Bhagavad Gita 6.6).

Consider this parable: A man walking through a dark forest held a lantern to light his path. Even when shadows loomed, the light kept him safe. Remembering the Master is like holding that lantern.

Dr. Hari: How should we view our worldly knowledge and ego?

Swamy: Do not be conceitful of your worldly knowledge, as it doesn't make you good. Don't exhibit such knowledge before the GURU to protect your ego. The GURU is compassionate but will always remain uncompromising with pride of his devotees.

"The humble sage, by virtue of true knowledge, sees with equal vision a learned and gentle Brahmin, a cow, an elephant, a dog, and a dog-eater" (Bhagavad Gita 5.18).

There's a parable about a wise sage who learned humility after being humbled by a simple villager's profound wisdom. True knowledge brings humility, not pride.

Dr. Hari: Why does it seem that the Master is absent during our crises?

Swamy: Understand that the Master is busily engaged in moulding your life, rectifying irreparable gaps. Like a washerman seems harsh while washing rugged clothes, the Master's process of cleansing is painful but gainful.

"In the stillness of the self, the Master's grace works silently, mending and guiding" (Guru Gita).

Consider this parable: A potter may seem rough while shaping clay, but he is creating a masterpiece. The Master's apparent harshness is part of our spiritual moulding.

Dr. Hari: How does the Master cure our inner diseases?

Swamy: By purifying our body, mind, and soul, making us pure and sacred. Be grateful to the Master by unconditionally surrendering yourself to His lotus feet.

"Just as a blazing fire turns firewood to ashes, the fire of knowledge burns to ashes all karma" (Bhagavad Gita 4.37).

There's a parable about a doctor who prescribed bitter medicine to cure a patient's illness. Though unpleasant, the medicine healed the patient. The Master's teachings may be tough, but they purify us.

Dr. Hari: What should our prayer to the Master be?

Swamy: Always say, "I love you, Master. I thank you, Master. Be with me forever, Master." This devotion will transmit His energy onto you, bringing transformation and the renaissance you seek.

"Devotion to the Master opens the doors to divine grace and inner transformation" (Guru Gita).

Consider this parable: A devotee's constant prayer and love for the Master were like magnets attracting divine grace, transforming his life completely. Our sincere prayers draw the Master's transformative energy.

A Conversation with Sri Vidyanarayana Theertha Swamiji: Insights into the Cosmic Essence

Introduction

In one of our enlightening dialogues with Sri Vidyanarayana Theertha of Badrika Peetam at our residence, profound insights into the cosmic essence and the interconnectedness of all life were shared. The conversation focused on transcending personal identity, embracing universal truths, and the deep bonds that connect us all.

Q&A Section with Parables and Examples

Question: Swamy, how can we transcend our personal identity and embrace a greater perspective?

Answer: Reflect deeply on your experiences and perceptions. Consider the essence behind your daily interactions and look beyond personal concerns to recognize the broader, universal connections that shape your existence. This shift in perspective helps you grasp your place within the vast cosmic order.

Parable: In the Bhagavad Gita, Arjuna's journey from confusion to enlightenment reflects this transcendence. By moving beyond his personal doubts and ego, he aligns with Krishna's cosmic perspective, realizing his true duty and place in the universe.

Question: What is the importance of relaxation in our spiritual journey?

Answer: Releasing tension revitalizes stagnant energy and helps you move beyond the ego. Genuine relaxation helps transcend the self, aligning with the expansive cosmic view.

Parable: In the Ramayana, Hanuman's devotion and calmness under pressure, such as during the search for Sita or the burning of Lanka, showcase how inner peace and relaxation enable one to achieve great feats and align with divine purpose.

Question: How can we understand the eternal connection that binds all beings?

Answer: Despite appearances of separation, the bond of love that connects all beings is eternal. Although it may seem there has been a long absence, the connection is constant.

Parable: The relationship between Lord Rama and his devotee Hanuman is a prime example. Despite physical separations and challenges, their bond of love and devotion remains unshakable, reflecting the eternal connection that transcends the material realm.

Question: How do we align with higher guidance in our daily lives?

Answer: Aligning with higher guidance involves embodying its teachings in everyday life. True alignment means living the guidance in both word and action.

Parable: In the Mahabharata, the Pandavas' adherence to dharma and their obedience to Krishna's guidance, despite numerous trials, exemplifies how aligning with divine wisdom and living according to higher principles leads to ultimate success and righteousness.

Question: How can we perceive beyond the external world and embrace the cosmic perspective?

Answer: Embark on an inner journey to perceive beyond the external world. The Earth rotates, yet the core essence remains still. Contemplate this paradox to see beyond illusions.

Parable: In the Vishnu Purana, Lord Vishnu's cosmic form, encompassing all creation and beyond, demonstrates the unchanging essence underlying the ever-changing universe. This perspective encourages us to look beyond the superficial and connect with the eternal truth.

Question: Why is it important to navigate transient desires and focus on enduring truths?

Answer: The transient allure of the world is insignificant compared to inner realization. Focusing on enduring truths brings lasting fulfilment.

Parable: The story of King Dhritarashtra in the Mahabharata highlights the consequences of attachment to worldly desires and power. His inability to relinquish his desires led to the downfall of his dynasty, emphasizing the importance of prioritizing spiritual growth over transient gains.

Question: How can we find inner peace amid the chaos of the world?

Answer: Cultivate inner peace through self-reflection and adherence to life's principles. This practice of inner tranquillity allows you to maintain focus and clarity amid external chaos.

Parable: In the Bhagavad Gita, Krishna advises Arjuna to find inner peace through self-discipline and detachment from the fruits of actions. This practice of inner tranquillity allows one to maintain focus and clarity amid external chaos.

Q: Why do problems exist in our lives?

A: Problems exist because we are not connected to the MASTER who is always with us and within us. The MASTER guides and guards us from all calamities and adversities in life. It is only when we realize this Truth that we can make rich contributions to society, glorify our existence, and make our lives more meaningful and purposeful.

Parable:

A disciple once complained to his Guru about the continuous challenges he faced. The Guru took him to a tree and asked him to hold a branch and hang from it. The disciple did as told, and after a while, he became tired and afraid. The Guru then said, "Let go." The disciple hesitated but eventually trusted his Guru and let go, only to find that he was just inches above the ground. The Guru explained, "Problems persist because you hold on to them. Trust in the Master, and you will realize that the ground is always near."

Q: How does awareness affect our lives?

A: Awareness about the powerful inner energy within us awakens our vibrant spirit. Each experience with our MASTER enriches our wisdom and endows us with the power of discrimination to live life in totality.

Parable:

A traveller lost in a dense forest panicked and felt hopeless. Suddenly, he remembered the compass his friend had given him. Using it, he found his way out of the forest. Similarly, our awareness is like that compass, guiding us out of confusion and darkness towards enlightenment and clarity.

Q: What role does the MASTER play in our lives?

A: The MASTER is the architect of our lives. There is nothing impossible for the MASTER. Therefore, we should not fear people or our surroundings, as none are as great as our MASTER. We should have unquestionable faith in the divine power of the MASTER, who weaves the fabric of our lives as He sees fit, regardless of our likes and dislikes.

Parable:

A potter was shaping a lump of clay into a beautiful vase. The clay resisted, wanting to stay in its original form. The potter gently said, "Trust in my hands. I know the design I have in mind for you." The clay surrendered, and soon it transformed into a masterpiece. Likewise, the MASTER shapes our lives with a divine design, even if we don't understand it at first.

Q: What should our attitude be towards the MASTER?

A: We are in the web of His grace. We should surrender to the Lotus Feet of the MASTER and serve Him with unconditional love without thinking about the past, present, or future. We are born to love Him and be loved by Him. Everything else is secondary and should not significantly affect our spirits.

Parable:

A bee buzzing around a flower garden found the perfect bloom and decided to stay there, drinking its nectar. It didn't worry about the other flowers it had left behind or the ones it might find in the future. It found contentment in the present bloom. Similarly, we should find contentment in serving our MASTER with love and devotion, without being distracted by past or future concerns.

Q: What should be our daily prayer?

A: Our daily prayer should be, "I Love You, Master," "I Thank You, Master," and "Bless Me, Master." This prayer should become a regular part of our lives.

Parable:

A thirsty crow found a pitcher with a little water at the bottom. Unable to reach it, the crow started dropping pebbles into the pitcher. Slowly, the water level rose, and the crow could drink it. Persistent prayer, like the crow's pebbles, gradually fills our lives with the Master's grace.

Q: How do we enter and exit the MASTER's domain?

A: We enter His DARBAR by virtue of the good deeds we have carried out in previous lives, as well as those we are carrying at present. We experience His unalloyed, unconditional, and unparalleled love and exit by becoming one with Him.

Parable:

A seed buried in the soil undergoes transformation, pushing through the dirt, sprouting into a sapling, and eventually blossoming into a tree. The journey through the soil is necessary for its growth. Similarly, our journey through life, guided by the MASTER's love, transforms us and ultimately leads us to merge with Him.

Our conversation with Sri Vidyanarayana Yathi offered profound insights into the cosmic essence and the interconnectedness of all life. The teachings emphasized the importance of transcending personal ego to align with a higher, universal perspective. By bending and mending our ego, we open ourselves to a deeper understanding and connection with the cosmic whole.

The journey to overcoming the self is not merely about intellectual realization but also about heartfelt transformation. As we embrace higher guidance and cultivate inner peace, we begin to navigate the complexities of existence with clarity and grace. This process allows us to harmonize our individual selves with the expansive cosmic order, leading to a more fulfilling and purposeful life.

Nature - God's Mirror Image

Nature is God's beautiful creation. God's mirror image exists in every speck of Nature. Hence, Nature is God, and God is Nature. They are inseparable and indistinguishable. Caring, loving, and becoming in tune with Mother Nature is equivalent to adoration for the Almighty, the owner of this Cosmos.

Nature exists in our body, bestowed by God. How beautiful is our body, which took its shape in the womb of Mother? Is not our body and its beautiful functioning mechanism a part of God's wonderful creation? Are we aware of this great miracle? The most merciful God has given us more than enough without any order. There are beautifully embedded teeth in the mouth to grind the food.

Acknowledging the Omnipresence of Nature

How often do we acknowledge the omnipresent Nature and the boundless energy it manifests in countless ways? Nature exists both within and outside of us. It resides within our intricately formed bodies, as well as in the external world—the starry sky, the earth, rivers, mountains, trees, and valleys.

True spiritual experiences unfold when we expand our perception from 'I am THIS' to 'I am THAT.' It's crucial to constantly remind ourselves that 'God is Nature, Nature is Mother, Mother is in me, and I am at her Feet.' Here, I share a brief conversation between my brother, Dr Hari, and Swamy Vidyanarayana Theertha, followed by the hidden meaning of it.

Dr. Hari: Swamy, how can we truly realize the divinity within Nature and within ourselves?

Swamy: To realize the divinity within Nature and within ourselves, we must cultivate a deep sense of awareness and reverence. Just as the river flows tirelessly towards the ocean, our spiritual journey should be one of continuous seeking and devotion. Reflect upon the teachings of the ancient epics and Puranas, where Nature is often depicted as a divine force.

Parable: The River and the Ocean

Consider the story of a small river that longed to merge with the ocean. Despite facing numerous obstacles—mountains, forests, and deserts—it never ceased its journey. Finally, it reached the ocean, losing its individual identity and becoming one with the vast expanse. Similarly, when we align ourselves with Nature, shedding our ego and worldly attachments, we merge with the divine consciousness.

The Hidden Meaning

The river represents our soul, and the ocean symbolizes the divine. The obstacles faced by the river are the challenges and distractions of life. The river's persistence and eventual merging with the ocean teach us about the importance of perseverance and faith in our spiritual journey. By recognizing the divinity in Nature and ourselves, we transcend our individual ego and realize our oneness with the divine essence.

Embracing the Cosmic Connection

The connection between Nature and God reminds us of the cosmic unity we are all part of. Embracing this connection brings us closer to understanding our true selves and the divine essence within us. As we nurture Nature, we nurture our souls, creating a harmonious balance that reflects the eternal bond between the Creator and creation.

May we always remember and cherish the divine reflection in Nature, recognizing that the presence of God is profoundly manifested in every leaf, every drop of water, and every breath we take.

Navigating the Complex Landscape of Modern Medicine: A Harmonious Blend of Science, Spirituality, and Compassion

In an era of unprecedented strides in modern medicine, the limitations of this field are increasingly apparent. Despite the remarkable advancements in technology and medical practices, the human body cannot be treated as a mere mechanical apparatus where parts can be replaced at will. The essence of human life is intricate and multifaceted, encompassing physical, mental, and spiritual dimensions that extend beyond the reach of conventional medicine.

The Pitfalls of Over-Specialization

One significant limitation of modern medicine is the tendency toward excessive specialization. While specialization has undeniably advanced our understanding of specific diseases, it often leads to a fragmented view of the human body. A doctor who focuses solely on one aspect of medicine may lose sight of the holistic nature of health, where mind and spirit are intertwined with the physical body. As Yukteswar Maharaj wisely said to Paramahamsa Yogananda, "You shall be well and strong," highlighting the profound connection between spiritual and physical well-being.

The Limitations of Medicine and the Boundless Potential of Divine Healing

Medicine, despite its advancements, has inherent limitations. It operates within a framework of scientific principles that, while effective, cannot encompass the boundless power of the Divine Life Force. This divine power, as illustrated by the miraculous events described by Paramahamsa Yogananda, transcends the boundaries of conventional medicine. Miracles, as described in spiritual teachings, defy natural laws and reveal a higher order of existence that modern science struggles to explain.

Jesus performed countless miracles, including healing the sick, raising the dead, and calming storms, vividly demonstrating His profound divine power and compassion. These acts reveal the boundless potential of divine intervention in the physical world and underscore a spiritual reality that transcends ordinary human experience.

A quite number of miracles of revered saints such as Mahavatar Babaji, Lahiri Mahasaya, Yukteswar Giri Maharaj, and Swami Yogananda highlight the remarkable ability of self-realized masters to channel divine energy for profound healing. These instances emphasize the existence of a realm beyond the physical, where divine energy and spiritual principles deeply influence our lives. They serve as powerful reminders that spiritual power and higher consciousness can significantly enhance our well-being and expand our understanding of the universe.

Saints and sages worldwide have exhibited remarkable healing abilities that defy scientific explanations. Their deep faith and spiritual insight are credited with their extraordinary healing abilities. Documented and undocumented instances demonstrate that the realm of divine healing encompasses a profound layer of existence, transcending the boundaries of traditional medical science.

The Role of Modern Science and the Concept of Maya

Modern science, while invaluable, is limited by its own parameters. It can elucidate the laws governing the physical universe but falls short when addressing the subtler, spiritual laws that govern the inner realms of consciousness. Newton's laws and Einstein's theories, while ground-breaking, operate within the confines of Maya—the illusion of the physical world. Sir James Jeans aptly remarked that the universe seems more like a "Great Thought" than a "Great Machine," emphasizing the shift from a mechanistic to a more holistic understanding of reality.

The Integration of Medicine, Spirituality, and Compassion

As a doctor, I have witnessed both the strengths and weaknesses of modern medicine. The pursuit of wealth in corporate hospitals often overshadows the fundamental principle of empathy. Patients should not be treated as commodities but as individuals deserving of compassion and understanding. A doctor's goal should not be financial gain but the ability to provide comfort and healing. The power of creating hope is immeasurable, whereas instilling fear can exacerbate suffering and lead to psychosomatic disorders.

In my personal experience, the limitations of medical science became glaringly evident when my loved ones suffered due to lapses in diagnosis and treatment. This experience reinforced the need for a holistic approach that integrates various healing traditions—homoeopathy, Ayurveda, Unani, Yoga, and Siddha. It is not about proving which method is superior but about finding effective solutions for those in need.

A Vision for the Future

I envision a future where patients are genuinely comforted, families find relief, and the relationship between doctors and patients mirrors that of empathetic parents and children. Technology should aid in solving medical problems, but the passion for medicine should be rooted in compassion and transformation. I extend my heartfelt gratitude to my professor, Dr. Rama Chandra Rao, whose compassionate heart and accurate diagnosis exemplify the ideal integration of medical expertise and empathy.

Conclusion

In the grand tapestry of existence, science, spirituality, and medicine are threads that weave together to form a holistic understanding of life and healing. By embracing this integration and acknowledging the miraculous healing power demonstrated by saints and sages, we can move towards a future where medical practice reflects the true essence of empathy and compassion, transforming both the lives of patients and the field of medicine itself.

Wisdom: Integrating Sanatana Dharma with Modern Management

This article is inspired by an enlightening exchange between my brother, Dr. Hari, and myself. Dr. Hari's extensive experience in management provided valuable insights into integrating the principles of Sanatana Dharma, the ancient wisdom of tradition, into contemporary management practices. Motivated by our discussion, I aim to share these insights with leaders across various disciplines, showcasing how Sanatana Dharma's timeless principles transcend technology, engineering, science, arts, commerce, and all branches of knowledge.

Sanatana Dharma: A Timeless Guide for Modern Management

Sanatana Dharma: Principles of Righteousness

Sanatana Dharma, often referred to as the ' tradition,' offers timeless principles that guide individuals toward a balanced and harmonious life. As Lord Krishna declares in the Bhagavad Gita, these principles are not mere relics of the past but serve as enduring guidance for ethical decision-making in management. They ensure that leadership, as the cornerstone of any organization, is rooted in moral integrity. This, in turn, fosters a balanced organizational culture where each member is respected and valued.

Acknowledgment of the Divine

Sanatana Dharma teaches us to recognize the divine presence in all beings, promoting universal respect and brotherhood. The Mahabharata, a significant text in Sanatana Dharma, exemplifies this through the story of Yudhishthira and the dog. As Yudhishthira prepares to enter heaven, he is asked to leave the dog behind. Despite the offer of bliss, he refuses to abandon his loyal companion, demonstrating profound compassion and loyalty. This act, rooted in the principles of 'Dharma' and 'Ahimsa' (non-violence), highlights the divine essence present in every being, fostering universal brotherhood.

In management, recognizing the intrinsic value of each team member cultivates a culture of respect and inclusiveness. As Mahatma Gandhi emphasized, "The best way to find yourself is to lose yourself in the service of others." By creating an environment where everyone feels valued, teamwork and collaboration thrive, enhancing overall productivity and morale.

Application in Management

1. **Promoting Respect and Inclusiveness:**

   - Acknowledging each individual's inherent worth fosters an environment of respect and open communication. This, in turn, promotes trust and mutual understanding among team members.

- Inclusiveness recognizes and appreciates diverse backgrounds and perspectives, leading to innovative solutions and enriched collaborative experiences.

2. **Enhancing Teamwork and Collaboration:**

- When team members feel respected, they are more likely to engage actively and contribute their best efforts, boosting teamwork and collaboration.

- Ensuring that all voices are heard and considered strengthens team cohesion and effectiveness.

3. **Building a Positive Work Culture:**

- A management approach that respects the divine essence in everyone nurtures a positive work culture where empathy and kindness are prioritized. This leads to improved job satisfaction and attracts and retains talent.

4. **Driving Organizational Success:**

- Organizations embodying respect and inclusiveness are more adaptable and resilient. They harness the full potential of their diverse teams, driving sustained growth and success.

Nurturing Knowledge and Wisdom

Sanatana Dharma values both worldly and spiritual knowledge. The Mundaka Upanishad beautifully articulates this balance: "Two kinds of knowledge must be known – that which is para vidya and that which is apara vidya. The apara vidya is in the Rig Veda, Yajur Veda, Sama Veda, and Atharva Veda texts. The para vidya is that by which the imperishable Brahman is attained" (MU 1.1.4-5). This distinction enlightens us about the importance of understanding both practical and transcendent wisdom.

In management, the pursuit of continuous learning and development is not just important, it's essential for innovation and adaptability. By integrating practical skills with deeper spiritual insights, leaders can approach challenges with greater wisdom and resilience, fostering a culture of growth and commitment.

Actions of Selflessness

The principle of Karma Yoga in Sanatana Dharma advocates for selfless action. Lord Krishna teaches, "You have the right to perform your prescribed duties, but you are not entitled to the fruits of your actions" (BG 2.47). This principle emphasizes serving others without attachment to outcomes. Effective managers who prioritize collective success over personal gain foster a culture of selflessness and shared purpose.

Truth as the Foundation

Truth (Satya) is a cornerstone of Sanatana Dharma. Upholding truth aligns one with divine will, as exemplified by King Harishchandra, who sacrificed everything to uphold truth. As he is quoted, "The truth is the light that guides the path of righteousness" (Mahabharata).

In management, transparency and honesty are crucial for building trust and credibility and essential for strong stakeholder relationships.

Harmony with Nature

Sanatana Dharma emphasizes living in harmony with nature. The Atharva Veda states, "The heavens and the earth, let them give strength to us. Let the waters and the plants give us health and wealth" (Atharva Veda 7.6). Adopting sustainable practices and promoting corporate social responsibility ensures that business activities positively impact the environment and society.

Ahimsa (Non-violence)

Ahimsa, or nonviolence, is central to Sanatana Dharma. Mahatma Gandhi's life and teachings exemplify nonviolence in thought, word, and action, fostering peace and harmony. He famously said, "The best way to find yourself is to lose yourself in the service of others." Promoting a respectful and nonviolent workplace culture in management reduces conflicts and enhances productivity.

Nurturing Virtues

Sanatana Dharma encourages virtues such as patience, tolerance, and forgiveness. Lord Rama's conduct in the Ramayana, characterized by immense patience and tolerance, exemplifies these virtues. As Lord Rama says, "The strength of the righteous lies in their patience and forgiveness" (Ramayana). Demonstrating these virtues in management helps leaders handle challenges effectively and maintain a positive organizational culture.

Adherence to Duty (Dharma)

Fulfilling one's duties with dedication aligns with Sanatana Dharma's principle of Dharma. The Bhagavad Gita states, "Better is one's own duty, though devoid of merit, than the duty of another well discharged" (BG 3.35). In management, clear role definitions and a strong sense of duty among team members ensure efficient operations and accountability.

Devotion (Bhakti)

Devotion (Bhakti) to one's work and organization enhances productivity and job satisfaction. The devotion of Prahlada to Lord Vishnu, as depicted in the Puranas, exemplifies how faith and commitment foster inner peace and growth. As Prahlada said, "True devotion lies in the sincerity of one's actions" (Puranas).

Holistic Development

Sanatana Dharma promotes holistic development, integrating physical, mental, emotional, and spiritual well-being. The Upanishads advocate for a balanced approach to life. In management, supporting employees' holistic development through wellness programs and work-life balance initiatives fosters a motivated and healthy workforce.

Awareness and Mindfulness

The Bhagavad Gita advises, "Perform all your actions with your mind concentrated on the Self, renouncing attachment and looking upon success and failure with an equal eye" (BG 2.48). Mindfulness enhances focus, decision-making, and stress management, contributing to a more effective work environment.

Respecting Wisdom

Respecting elders' wisdom and scripture teachings enriches organizational knowledge. The Mahabharata states, "By serving the wise and elderly, one attains longevity, wisdom, fame, and strength" (MB 5.39). Valuing senior members' experience and insights enhances strategic planning and decision-making.

Meditation and Contemplation

Meditation and contemplation help calm the mind and enhance self-awareness. The Yoga Sutras state, "Yoga is the cessation of the modifications of the mind" (YS 1.2). Encouraging these practices among employees improves mental clarity, emotional stability, and overall well-being.

Attainment of Moksha

The ultimate goal of Sanatana Dharma is Moksha or liberation. This state of peace and bliss is achieved through the realization of oneness with the divine. As the Bhagavad Gita describes, "Having attained this state, he does not again fall into delusion" (BG 6.15). In management, striving for excellence while maintaining ethical integrity reflects the pursuit of Moksha, leading to enduring impact and legacy.

Spirituality: The Essence of Reality

Spirituality transcends religious boundaries and embodies universal truths. Embracing Sanatana Dharma's wisdom offers a comprehensive approach to addressing societal challenges. By integrating spirituality into personal and professional realms, we create a harmonious world where wisdom guides our actions, enriching all aspects of life.

Echoes of Grace: A Journey of Spiritual Discovery

The concept of the soul's journey and meeting individuals for specific purposes reflects a deeper spiritual understanding of life's interconnectedness and purpose. In the spiritual realm, each soul embarks on a unique journey towards growth, enlightenment, and fulfilling its higher purpose. This journey often intertwines with the journeys of others, leading to significant encounters that shape destinies and catalyze spiritual evolution.

Swami Vivekananda's life is a poignant example. Born as Narendra Nath Datta, he was destined to meet Sri Ramakrishna Paramahamsa, whose divine guidance and teachings profoundly influenced Vivekananda's spiritual path. Swami Ramakrishna recognized Vivekananda's potential and played a pivotal role in nurturing his spiritual awakening and mission.

Their meeting exemplifies the idea that souls often come together not by chance but as part of a greater plan. Ramakrishna's role as Vivekananda's spiritual *guide and mentor illustrates how individuals are interconnected in their spiritual quests. Vivekananda, in turn, carried forward Ramakrishna's teachings and established the Ramakrishna Mission to spread Vedanta philosophy and serve humanity.*

The importance of such soul connections lies in their transformative power. These encounters can awaken dormant potentials, inspire profound realizations, and propel individuals toward their life's purpose. They remind us that our lives are intertwined with others in ways that contribute to collective spiritual growth and the realization of divine truths.

Therefore, recognizing and honouring these soul connections and their purposes can deepen one's spiritual journey, offering clarity, purpose, and a sense of interconnectedness with the divine plan unfolding through human lives.

Sree lekha's Divine Journey

Sree Lekha's life is akin to a special thread woven by God. Born in Kambalapalli, a remote village in Sri Sathya Sai District, she faced adversity. Her encounter with my brother in KOGIRA Village during high school changed her life. Despite hardships, she carried strength and a determined spirit. Even in sorrow, hope shimmered in her eyes.

My brother sensed a deeper connection to our spiritual community, which moved her to tears upon

his departure. This bond deepened her curiosity to seek his guidance for her academic challenges. With support from the organization where my brother worked, she completed her diploma and graduated in Electrical Engineering. Her skin ailment, which was treated by our family homeopathic doctor, Dr Kumaraiah, further cemented her bond with our home, Kovela.

Guided by Divine Providence

Her arrival at Kovela was no coincidence but part of God's plan. She brought care in her smiles, clarity in her thoughts, purity in her heart, honesty in her words, and godliness in her actions. Finding peace at Kovela, she made it her sanctuary, embodying harmony and devotion. She became integral to our home, resonating with OM within our hearts.

Divine Revelations: The Sacred Path of Lekha and the Bonds of Destiny

In reverence, her family honours the AKKA DEVATALU. In the neighbouring village of KOGIRA, a lady divinely possessed by AKKAMMA DEVATA resides, offering guidance and insights. During one such possession, it was revealed that those destined to enter Lekha's life would ensure her well-being and education. These events preceding Lekha's presence in our lives underscore their profound significance, seemingly woven by divine hands.

I shared my life's intricacies with her, convinced of her divine nature and the cosmic purpose behind our bond. Engaging in spiritual readings of texts like SAI CHARITRA and teachings of RAMA KRISHNA PARAMAHAMSA with my brother, Dr. Hari, she became part of our SATSANG, generating positive vibrations during our family's trials. We felt she was heaven-sent, filling a void in our lives.

A Beacon of Light in Challenging Times

During COVID-19, she moved from her hostel to stay with us for online classes. Her presence brought joy amidst uncertainty. Encouraged by her noble family, who view our home as sacred, she shared wisdom beyond her years. Her journey isn't just about academic pursuits but about spiritual growth under God's guidance, teaching us resilience and faith.

Embracing Tradition and Spirituality

At Kovela, she learned cooking and cleanliness and embodied the spirit of OM, a sacred symbol representing the divine connection. She embraced English and manners, reflecting her inner grace. Her attire, akin to Sai Nivedita's sister, reflects her love for tradition and spirituality. Despite challenges from skeptical maids, she remained steadfast in her beliefs, a testament to her strength and humility.

A Bond of Love and Spiritual Kinship

In the evenings, deep conversations fostered a bond of love and spirituality. Strolling through her college campus, discussions on true friendship resonated. In Twilight's embrace, I asked her to support my brother as a beacon in his darkness. We felt deeply connected in those moments, bound by love, faith, and spiritual kinship. May she carry these sacred teachings, guided by OM's light in her journey.

A Soul Seeking Enlightenment

Sree Lekha transcends mere existence; she embodies a soul on a path toward enlightenment, a beacon of hope for us all. Her life unfolds like a divine tapestry, weaving threads of faith, strength, and personal growth. May her journey inspire all around her, guiding them to navigate life with grace and gratitude. May we be assured that we are all integral parts of God's grand design.

A Soul Seeking Enlightenment Sree Lekha transcends mere existence; she embodies a soul on a path toward enlightenment, a beacon of hope for us all. Her life unfolds like a divine tapestry, weaving threads of faith, strength, and personal growth. May her journey inspire all around her, guiding them to navigate life with grace and gratitude. May we be assured that we are all integral parts of God's grand design (After this para, run the following)

***

A Divine Bond Beyond Time

The Precious Gem

Love's Silent Tears
Love melted into tears, like a soft, gentle stream,
She was a lost gem, not merely a fleeting dream.
In every tear, compassion, so profound and deep,
Her silent pain was one our hearts could only weep.

A Timeless Connection
No words were needed, just emotions shared clear,
Her humble grace forged a bond both old and near.
I patted her back as if touched by heaven's grace,
A connection so profound, transcending time
and space.

The Healing Presence
She cried silently, her pain was hard to bear,
Her tears spoke volumes, revealing a heart laid bare.
A mini goddess with healing in her gaze,
Her presence a balm, soothing our troubled days.

Restoring Lives
She revived the lives that were slipping away,
Her eyes connected with our mother's celestial sway.
Her looks mirrored our sister's tender grace,
A touch that calmed our hearts, an embrace of solace.

A Radiant Embrace
With folded hands, she enveloped us in light,
Her pure love shining, making darkened paths bright.

Her memory lingers, her face etched in time,
A village girl, yet divine, a presence so sublime.

Eternal Understanding
Soul bonds transcend, where physical ties decay,
Her presence felt timeless, guiding our way.
She senses our wounds, as if knowing us before,
A deep understanding, that words could not explore.

The Sacred Arrival
She entered our hearts before she crossed our door,
Bringing the sacred OM, a silent, sacred roar.
Who is she, this gem so rare and true?
A blessing, a bond that forever renews.

Soulful Reflections: Embracing Truth in Everyday Moments

1

Journeying Through the Cosmos to Discover Your Inner Light"

Dear Sree Lekha,

As I reflect on the beauty and wisdom of the universe, I am compelled to share with you the profound insights that have touched my heart.

In this vast cosmos, every element, creature, and moment is a manifestation of God's divine plan. Our journey through this existence is akin to enrolling in the Universal University of Learning, where each experience is a lesson, and each encounter is an opportunity for growth.

From the gentle sway of the trees to the diligent labour of the ants, from the majestic flight of birds to the serene flow of rivers, every aspect of nature whispers its secrets to those willing to listen. In embracing nature's grandeur, we are reminded of our humble place in the grand scheme of creation.

To truly understand and appreciate the teachings of this divine university, one must approach with humility, an open mind, and a sincere desire to learn. Through this receptivity, we can unlock the boundless wisdom surrounding us and embark on a journey of spiritual enlightenment.

May you find inspiration and guidance in the teachings of the universe, and may your journey through this sacred school of life be filled with wonder, growth, and divine grace.

"Silence is higher than speech." In a society overwhelmed by noise, I pay homage to the goddess of wisdom, Saraswati, through the vow of silence. In this age of action, true wealth lies not in material possessions but in love and inner peace. "By silence, you will be with yourself. Through silence, you are yourself."

With Best Wishes

Dr C. Nagaraj

2

Another Year of Radiance: Celebrating Sree Lekha's Birthday

Dear Sree Lekha,

I hope this message finds you well. I wanted to share some heartfelt sentiments on your special day today.

As you celebrate another year of life, I want to extend my warmest wishes for joy and blessings. It's a remarkable day, coinciding with a Sunday and the new moon, marking the day of your birth. It holds a special significance, and I think of you fondly.

You are a radiant presence in our lives, bringing happiness and laughter wherever you go. I treasure the memories we've created together, from light-hearted moments to meaningful conversations about our dear mother. Your place in her heart is irreplaceable, and your presence brings immense joy to our family.

As you embark on another year of your journey, I encourage you to embrace opportunities for growth and strive for excellence. Remember, you are never alone; we are here to support and uplift you every step of the way.

Today, as we celebrate your birthday, let's make it a day filled with joy, gratitude, and togetherness. Let's take a moment to express gratitude to our parents for their love and sacrifices and revel in the warmth of family bonds.

With Best Wishes

Dr Nagaraj

3

Innocence: A Reflection of the Divine

Dear Sree Lekha,

Reflecting on childhood innocence, I am struck by its profound spiritual significance. A child is often said to be a reflection of God, embodying purity and divine simplicity.

In a child's world, there is a purity untouched by the complexities of adulthood. Play is their language, and toys are their universe. Within this innocence lies the essence of Godhood, undisturbed by the intellect that later clouds our perception.

As we journey through life, the demands of the world often pull us away from this innate purity. We become entangled in the busyness of adulthood, losing sight of the divine simplicity we once knew.

Yet, amidst the chaos, let us pause and recollect our childhood days. Let us remember the joy of playfulness and our profound connection to the divine in those moments of innocence. Tomorrow, Sai Leela is leaving. We feel your absence as a profound void.

As we navigate the complexities of adulthood, let us strive to preserve that Godly innocence within us. Let us pray to God to protect it from being shaded and faded by the challenges of life.

"Innocence is God." Let us hold onto this truth and cultivate the purity of heart that connects us to the divine. Whatever you touch turns to gold, as you were born with divine providence.

"You are your own strength!... Your description of your stay in your native village reflects rural innocence... It appears in your nicely mentioned words!...

Everyone should read this... It's very good to read

Your absence makes us feel very empty...

There's no moment without thinking of you!...

Sai Leela also comes to mind...

Whenever you come and serve us, feel that you are doing service to God!

Enjoy your stay in your village; we look forward to listening to KAMBALAPALLI Stories.

I put here a saying, 'If one wants to eat, they should eat green MIRAPAKAYA BAJJI (It is made of Green Chilli); if one wants to listen, they should listen to KAMABALAPALLI Stories from you"

With Best wishes

Dr Nagaraj

4

Crafting Beauty: A Journey Through Art, Athletics, and Creativity

Dear Sai Leela

You are a profoundly creative soul, an artist at heart, skilled in the delicate strokes of painting, the artistry of photography, and the grace of capturing nature's beauty through your lens.

Furthermore, you possess the athleticism and endurance of a dedicated runner, exuding sportsmanship and vigour in all your endeavours.

Continue honing your drawing and painting skills, allowing your imagination to soar and your talents to blossom on canvas.

Explore the realm of cinematography, masterfully crafting visual narratives and thematic animations using mobile applications, each frame a testament to your artistic vision.

Embrace the art of videography with finesse, weaving together moments of beauty and emotion into captivating visual stories that resonate deeply with your audience.

Dr Nagaraj

5

Sai Leela: Where Creativity Flourishes

Dear Sai Leela,

I hope this letter finds you in good health and high spirits. I trust you enjoy your online classes and spending quality time with your parents.

Your dedication to your studies and the joy you find in learning is truly inspiring. It warms our hearts to see you fully immersed in your studies, singing, dancing, and even enjoying movies. Your enthusiasm for life is contagious, reminding us to cherish every moment.

As you navigate your daily routine, remember to cherish each moment as a precious opportunity. Embrace every experience with awareness and gratitude, for every moment is a chance to connect with the divine.

Speaking of which, I hope you're relishing your time in Kambala Palli. I can imagine you spending time with our family, indulging in delicious meals prepared by Shree Lekha, and enjoying the serene surroundings. Consider taking some time for yourself amidst your busy schedule by practising some techniques shared by Shree Lekha.

Continue to read, study, and assist others as you always do. Keep singing, playing, and dancing with joy. Your presence brings us so much happiness, and we are truly grateful for you.

Sending you lots of love and best wishes for your continued success and happiness.

With love and contemplation,

Dr. Nagaraj

6

Dear Sree Lekha

From the realm of the gods, a divine maiden has arrived...

A divine yogi like you, what can I say to you? Offering gratitude 🙏 is not enough...

Are there any other virtuous souls like you among millions of people?

Encountering someone like you, blessed with divine qualities, is a blessing...

Surrendering to the Divine Essence of Sri Rama and Hanuman

Remembering you a lot

With Best Wishes

Dr C Nagaraj

7

Divine Encounters: Surrendering to Sri Rama and Hanuman's Essence

Dear Sri Lekha,

With the grace of the Divine, I pen this letter to you, hoping it finds you immersed in the serenity of spiritual bliss. As we approach the sacred juncture of our existence, my soul feels drawn to contemplate the profound essence encapsulated by Sri Rama and Hanuman. In the tapestry of our spiritual heritage, the intertwining threads of Dharma and Rama weave a divine narrative, illuminating the path of righteousness for seekers of truth. Sri Rama, the epitome of virtue and righteousness, serves as the divine embodiment of Dharma itself. His life, enshrined in the scriptures, resonates with timeless wisdom, guiding us towards the truth.

In the sacred annals of devotion, Hanuman's name shines as a radiant beacon of unwavering love and selfless service. His boundless devotion to Sri Rama transcends the realms of mortal comprehension, symbolizing the pinnacle of Bhakti and surrender. In the temple of our hearts, Hanuman stands guard, a sentinel of devotion, reminding us of the transformative power of love.

As we stand on the threshold of divine revelation, let us immerse ourselves in the divine essence of Sri Rama and Hanuman. Let their divine presence permeate every facet of our existence, illuminating the path of our spiritual journey with the radiant light of truth and devotion.

May this auspicious time be adorned with the fragrance of divine love, and may our souls resonate with the celestial melody of Sri Rama and Hanuman's grace. With heartfelt reverence and spiritual yearning,

Dr Nagaraj

8

Open Hearts, Open Minds: Navigating Meaningful Conversations

Dear Sree Lekha,

I hope this letter finds you in good spirits. I wanted to take a moment to express my thoughts and feelings with you.

Firstly, thank you for your openness and honesty in our recent conversations. It is refreshing to engage in discussions with someone who values sincere communication and thoughtful reflection.

During our last conversation, the topic of consuming non-vegetarian food arose, and I appreciated your perspective. You clearly have a strong conviction in your beliefs, which I greatly respect. However, I also wanted to share some of my thoughts with you.

You mentioned that someone argued in favour of non-vegetarianism, and my response was perceived as violent. I understand how my words may have come across as strong, and I apologize if I caused any discomfort. I intended not to impose my beliefs on those who are lovers of non-vegetarianism but to shed light on a different perspective.

When we discuss topics like dietary choices, it's important to approach them with empathy and understanding. Every individual has their own reasons for their choices, and it's crucial to respect those differences while engaging in meaningful dialogue.

Our actions have consequences, not just for ourselves but for the world around us. Whether it's the food we eat or the decisions we make, each choice we make has an impact, and it's essential to consider the implications of those choices.

In saying this, I encourage you to continue exploring your beliefs and values and always remain open to new perspectives. Through this openness and willingness to learn, we can grow as individuals and as a community.

Thank you once again for the opportunity to share my thoughts with you. I look forward to continuing our conversations and learning from each other.

Best wishes

Dr.Nagaraj

9

Sacred Reflections: Exploring the Teachings of Bhagawan Sri Ramana Maharshi

Dear Sree Lekha,

I trust this letter envelops you in the gentle embrace of spiritual consciousness. I wish to share my reflections on Bhagawan Sri Ramana Maharshi's profound teachings, whose wisdom illuminates the path of self-realization.

In contemplating the essence of the soul, Bhagawan Sri Ramana Maharshi leads us to the sublime understanding of Atma Tatvam. The Atma, the Self, transcends the transient nature of the physical and the fluctuating states of the mind. Through Atma Vicharana, the practice of self-inquiry, we embark on a journey to rediscover our innate divinity and abide in the unchanging truth of our being.

As you tread the sacred terrain of spiritual exploration, it is vital to cultivate humility and surrender. By relinquishing the ego's grip and surrendering to the divine will, we open ourselves to the boundless grace that guides our every step. We find liberation in the depths of surrender, for it is in surrendering that we truly gain.

Remember, dear Sree Lekha, that the spiritual journey is not merely a solitary endeavour but a divine communion. As you engage in introspection and self-discovery, may you feel the presence of the divine guiding you, comforting you, and illuminating your path with divine light. Om Sri Anjaneyaswami Namaha, invoking the blessings of Lord Hanuman to fortify your resolve and protect you on your spiritual odyssey. With heartfelt blessings

Dr Nagaraj

10

Ekadashi Blessings: Celebrating the Presence of Sri Ram

Dear Sree Lekha,

On this auspicious occasion of Ekadashi in May, I extend heartfelt greetings to you.

Sri Ramachandra incarnated in the Treta Yuga era, and Sri Krishna manifested in the Dwapara Yuga era. In this present age, we witness the extraordinary, timeless form, the embodiment of the four Vedas, the primal form of the Supreme Brahman—Bhagawan Sri Ram, the unparalleled avatar.

On this divine occasion of celebrating Bhagawan Sri Ram's appearance day, I convey my sincerest wishes to you.

With affection

Dr Nagaraj

11

"Night's Divine Whisper: Moonlight and Starshine"

Dear Sree Lekha,

As I sit under the canopy of the night sky, enveloped in the gentle glow of the moonlight, I am reminded of this celestial display's profound spiritual insights.

With its soft radiance, the moon symbolizes the divine presence that illuminates our path in life. Just as the moon reflects the light of the sun, guiding us through the darkness of the night, the divine light within each of us guides us through the challenges and uncertainties of our spiritual journey.

In the quiet stillness of the night, as I gaze upon the twinkling stars, I am reminded of the interconnectedness of all creation. Like a beacon of light in the vast expanse of the universe, each star represents a soul on its unique journey. And yet, despite our paths, we are all united in the cosmic dance of existence, bound together by the divine energy that flows through us all.

As I commune with the stars, I feel a deep reverence and awe for the divine presence that permeates all creation. In their silent wisdom, the stars remind me of the importance of humility and gratitude on the spiritual path. Only when we surrender our ego and acknowledge the divine within and around us can we truly experience life's profound beauty and interconnectedness.

12

Journey to Enlightenment: A Guiding Light Amid Life's Adventures

Dear Sree Lekha,

I trust this letter finds you well. Today, I wish to share a profound, resonated truth: "Seeking enlightenment is the sole purpose of life."

We encounter various experiences, challenges, and opportunities in our journey through this world. Yet amidst the hustle and bustle of everyday life, it is essential to remember the ultimate goal—to seek enlightenment, attain a higher state of consciousness, and realise our existence's true nature.

As we navigate life's ups and downs, let us keep sight of this fundamental truth. Let us strive to cultivate wisdom, compassion, and inner peace, knowing that these qualities lead us closer to enlightenment.

May this reminder serve as a guiding light on your spiritual journey, illuminating the path ahead and inspiring you to seek the highest truth in all that you do.

With warm regards and heartfelt wishes,

Dr Nagaraj

13

Moonlit Reflections: Embracing the Sacred Gift of Each Moment

Dear Sree Lekha,

On moonlit nights, as I immerse myself in the beauty of the cosmos, I am reminded to cherish each moment as a sacred gift and remain ever-mindful of the divine presence surrounding us.

With heartfelt blessings

Dr. Nagaraj

14

Sacred Reflections: A Letter of Spiritual Wisdom

Dear Raghavendra

In the gentle embrace of silence amidst the whispers of the wind and the rustle of leaves, I find solace in the timeless wisdom that surrounds us. Like a sacred gift bestowed upon us, each moment holds the potential for spiritual growth and enlightenment.

As we journey through the labyrinth of life, may we pause to listen to the quiet echoes of our inner selves, for therein lies the profound truths that guide us towards understanding and compassion. Let us light the lamp of awareness in the darkness of ignorance, illuminating the path for ourselves and those around us.

In the vast expanse of existence, may we find unity in diversity, recognizing the divine spark that resides within each soul. Let us embrace the journey with humility and gratitude, knowing that every experience, whether joyous or challenging, is a stepping stone towards higher consciousness. As we navigate the ebbs and flows of life, may we cultivate kindness, love, and empathy, for these virtues truly connect with the essence of our being? Let us strive to be beacons of light in a world often shrouded in darkness, spreading hope and understanding wherever we go.

Let us commune with the divine in the silence of our hearts, finding strength, solace, and inspiration in its boundless grace. For in the stillness, we discover the infinite depths of our soul, and therein lies the key to unlocking the mysteries of existence.

With heartfelt blessings and warm wishes,

Dr Nagaraj

15

Innocence Unveils Divinity: Rediscovering the Sacred Essence Within

Dear Sree Lekha,

I hope this letter finds you well. I wanted to share some reflections with you, inspired by the profound truth that "Child is like God; Child is God." This sentiment resonates deeply, reminding us of the pure innocence and divine essence that children embody.

In childhood, we glimpse a reflection of Godhood. It's a time when innocence reigns supreme when the world is seen through eyes untainted by cynicism or doubt. Play is the language of the child, and toys are their universe. In this state of being, there is a connection to something sacred, something inherently divine.

Yet, as we grow older, something changes. Intellect creeps in, and with it, innocence slips away. It's as though there's a trade-off between the two: where intellect enters, innocence exits. The world becomes more complex and more demanding, and we find ourselves caught up in its web.

But amidst the hustle and bustle of life, let us not forget the purity of our childhood selves. Let us remember the days when playfulness was our only concern, the world was simpler, and our hearts lighter. It's a time to pause and reflect, to reconnect with that inner innocence that is still within us, waiting to be rediscovered.

So, let us take a moment to ponder and pray. Let us pray that our Godly innocence remains intact and that it is not overshadowed or lost amidst the noise of the world. For in innocence, we find a glimpse of God, a reminder of something sacred and pure. "Innocence is God." May we always hold onto that truth, and may it guide us on our journey through life.

With best wishes

With heartfelt blessings and warm wishes,

Dr Nagaraj

16

Basking in Surya's Grace: Reflections on Rathasaptami and Nature's Teachings

Dear Sree Lekha,

I hope this letter finds you in good spirits. Today marks a special occasion, the auspicious Rathasaptami, dedicated to the worship of Surya Deva, the radiant Sun God. On this day, as we bask in the glory of the Sun, let us take a moment to reflect on the profound teachings that nature and its celestial embodiment offer us.

The Sun, often revered as the life source and life force of our cosmos, holds within its brilliance the essence of health and vitality. It is the giver of energy, the orchestrator of seasons, and the custodian of days and nights. Indeed, the celestial beauty that surrounds us finds its ultimate expression in the nurturing warmth of the Sun's rays.

Just as a mother is our first teacher, Mother Nature is our greatest mentor. It whispers lessons of humility, gratitude, and interconnectedness, inviting us to learn from its boundless wisdom. Yet, in our relentless pursuit of progress, we often overlook these teachings, consumed by our own self-interest and mechanical routines.

The chariot of Surya Deva, drawn by seven horses, symbolizes the seven colours of the radiant Sun. Each hue represents a facet of its divine energy, reminding us of the intricate tapestry of creation woven by nature's hand.

A mystery transcends scientific understanding in the vast expanse of the solar realm. It is a realm where yoga merges with worship, where the Sun's sterilizing and cleansing powers mirror the purity of the soul. Solar energy electrifies, enshrines, enlightens, and enlivens, serving as a testament to the boundless potential of divine energy.

As we pay homage to Surya Deva on this sacred day, let us do so with hearts filled with thankfulness and souls brimming with gratitude. Let us remember that every element of nature, from the smallest ant to the mightiest elephant, is a teacher in its own right, offering us invaluable lessons in humility and appreciation.

In closing, let us always remember the importance of gratitude. For there is no greater sin than ingratitude and no greater virtue than expressing thanks to nature and the divine with sincerity and reverence.

Wishing you a blessed Rathasaptami filled with the warmth and radiance of Surya Deva's divine grace.

With heartfelt memories

Dr Nagaraj

17

Embracing Life's Complexity: Navigating with Strength and Wisdom

Dear Sree Lekha,

Navigating the complexities of the world and its people can indeed be challenging. Feeling frustrated when things don't go as expected or when faced with situations beyond our comprehension is natural. However, it's essential to remember that life is a mix of pleasure and pain, and there's often wisdom to be found in both.

Finding balance amidst life's complexities involves embracing both joy and hardship. Sometimes, what brings pleasure may also bring pain, and vice versa. It's crucial to remain grounded and not be swayed by superficial attractions or fleeting distractions.

Drawing strength from the love and blessings of those who care for you, like Hari sir and your noble family, can provide comfort and guidance along life's journey. Remember to take time to relax, rejuvenate, and reflect on your path. While it's important to strive towards your goals, it's equally important to cherish moments of peace and connection, such as being in the embrace of a loving mother.

Ultimately, trust in your inner strength and resilience to navigate life's complexities. Stay true to your values, remain open to growth and learning, and trust that you will reach your destiny with grace and purpose. Bhagawan Sri Ramana Maharshi is the Ultimate—the essence of the soul, the inquiry into the self—transcending the body and mind, residing in the state of the self. As you tread on this divine path, you are journeying spiritually.

Om Sri Anjeyaswami Namah."

Dr Nagaraj

18

Journeying with Focus: Mindful Strategies for Exam Success

Dear Sri Lekha,

Congratulations on completing your first exam with excellence! You've set a great precedent for the exams to come. Keep up the fantastic work!

I want to share some insights with you, inspired by daily life's chaotic yet profound experiences. In the noisy weather of the college bus, amidst the cacophony of voices and distractions, there lies a profound truth about the dualities of human existence. In the midst of chaos, it's essential to maintain our ethos, inner calm, and integrity while chaos may surround us.

It's often best to ignore and forgive when faced with disturbances and distractions. Understand that others' actions are a reflection of their own inner world, and it's not our place to judge or engage with negativity. Instead, focus on occupying a peaceful space for yourself, whether it's physically on the bus or mentally in your mind.

As you journey towards your exam centre, let your focus be unwavering on your studies. Engage in practices like reading or memorizing material to keep your mind sharp and prepared. Enchanting prayers or mantras can also provide psychological strength and focus.

Remember, noisy scenes may attract unwanted attention and negative energy. Stay focused on your goals and detach yourself from distractions. Every moment is precious, so make the best use of your time.

Be like a yogini, finding inner peace amidst external chaos. Embrace the role of a philosopher, seeking wisdom and understanding in every experience. Be a witness to the world around you, observing without attachment.

Be a witness to the chaotic dance of illusion, paying attention to the distorted perspectives and opposing actions.

Focus solely on your studies, your subject, your exam—nothing else, nothing else.

Remain vigilant, cautious, and detached. Stay dissociated from distractions.

Don't squander even a single minute. Mentally practice Bhramari Pranayama.

Invoke intuition. Invoke God. Then, answer the questions one by one calmly and quietly.

When your aim is high, let go of what is insignificant. Who are those who relate to your soul?

Think of your soul. Think of your goal.

Achieve victory and success.

With best wishes

Dr Nagaraj

19

United Against Adversity: A Call to Action in the Face of the Pandemic

Dear Sreelekha,

I hope this letter finds you well amidst these challenging times. As we navigate through the trials posed by the pandemic, we must remain informed and proactive in our efforts to combat it.

The images and messages shared regarding the current situation underscore the urgency of the matter. The list of vaccines awaiting approval from the DCGI presents a beacon of hope in our battle against the virus. These vaccines must receive timely approval to bolster our defences and mitigate the spread of the virus.

My observations regarding the causes of the current spike in cases resonate deeply. Carelessness, recklessness, and negligence have undoubtedly contributed to our predicament. It is essential for each of us to strictly adhere to pandemic guidelines, including wearing face masks, practising frequent hand hygiene, and maintaining social distancing. The emphasis on vaccine acceptance cannot be overstated. Developed domestically, vaccines such as Covishield and Covaxin have demonstrated both efficacy and safety. Overcoming vaccine hesitancy is crucial for achieving widespread immunity and ultimately overcoming the pandemic. In these trying times, our collective resilience and unity will see us through. Let us continue to support one another, remain vigilant in our efforts to curb the spread of the virus, and embrace the opportunity to get vaccinated when it becomes available. Take care and stay safe.

Dr Nagaraj

About the Writer

Dr. C. Hari holds advanced degrees, including a Master of Philosophy and a Doctor of Philosophy in Rural Development. With a decade of research experience, his focus has been on leadership, rural entrepreneurship, and community organization. He is passionate about writing and has contributed articles in both English and Telugu.

Dr. Hari served as the Director of Monitoring & Evaluation (M&E) and Projects at RDT, which was established in 1969, for 32 years. In addition to his role at RDT, he trains development workers in non-profit organizations on Planning, Monitoring, and Evaluation (PME), Gender, and Leadership.

A prolific writer and musician, Dr. Hari has composed over 200 songs on various themes and is skilled in playing the Tabala. His Telugu album dedicated to mothers has gained significant popularity, amassing over 1.42 million views on YouTube.

The current book depicts the sacred soul of a remarkable individual who, apart from his medical career, taught at the Government Medical College in Anantapur for over 20 years. He wrote countless poems covering themes such as gods, society, and nature. His compassion and love for nature are well-known, and he has embarked on an extensive spiritual journey, traveling with several saints. Despite his profound insights and experiences, he remains a humble figure, never disclosing his identity.

He is grounded and firmly believes that true spirituality transcends religious dogmas, aligning with his philosophy that Truth is God. His realist perspective and dedication to this truth have been central to his life and work. The book offers genuine insights derived from years of research, diary entries, and interactions with his brother, Dr. C. Nagaraj. It provides readers with an understanding of various perspectives, including spiritual aspirations, presenting facts that reflect actual occurrences rather than illusions or imaginations.